T0351026

Mastering KDE

Mastering KDE helps the reader master the KDE desktop environment for a faster and more robust computing experience.

The best thing about Linux is the plethora of choices that users tend to get. Whether it pertains to the kernel modules, or to the desktop environments, there is no shortage of options.

Speaking of desktop environments, KDE stands tall as one of the leading options.

KDE stands for K Desktop Environment, an open source desktop working platform featuring a graphical user interface (GUI). When KDE was first introduced, it was known as the Kool desktop environment, later reduced to KDE. The KDE GUI includes everything a typical user would require, such as a file manager, window manager, help tool, and system settings. KDE is the default desktop environment for various Linux distros, and also has its own flagship distro, KDE Neon, that is covered at length in *Mastering KDE*.

KDE comes with features that give users remote access to other devices, such as computers running Windows, Linux, macOS, or Android smartphones. KDE Connect, a Linux-based application, is one such solution that allows users to transfer data between multiple devices and operate them remotely. This book talks about everyday usage of KDE, including remote access and KDE development.

With *Mastering KDE*, using KDE for day-to-day computing becomes simple and straightforward, which will undoubtedly help readers boost their productivity.

The *Mastering Computer Science* series is edited by Sufyan bin Uzayr, a writer and educator with over a decade of experience in the computing field.

Mastering Computer Science
Series Editor: Sufyan bin Uzayr

Mastering KDE: A Beginner's Guide
Jaskiran Kaur, Mathew Rooney, and Shahryar Raz

Mastering Flutter: A Beginner's Guide
Divya Sachdeva, NT Ozman, and Reza Nafim

Mastering Vue.js: A Beginner's Guide
Lokesh Pancha, Divya Sachdeva, and Faruq KC

Mastering GoLang: A Beginner's Guide
Divya Sachdeva, D Nikitenko, and Aruqqa Khateib

Mastering Ubuntu: A Beginner's Guide
Jaskiran Kaur, Rubina Salafey, and Shahryar Raz

Mastering Visual Studio Code: A Beginner's Guide
Jaskiran Kaur, D Nikitenko, and Mathew Rooney

For more information about this series, please visit: https://www.routledge
.com/Mastering-Computer-Science/book-series/MCS

The "Mastering Computer Science" series of books are authored by the Zeba Academy team members, led by Sufyan bin Uzayr.

Zeba Academy is an EdTech venture that develops courses and content for learners primarily in STEM fields, and offers education consulting to Universities and Institutions worldwide. For more info, please visit https://zeba.academy

Mastering KDE
A Beginner's Guide

Edited by
Sufyan bin Uzayr

CRC Press
Taylor & Francis Group
Boca Raton London New York

CRC Press is an imprint of the
Taylor & Francis Group, an **informa** business

First Edition published 2023
by CRC Press
6000 Broken Sound Parkway NW, Suite 300, Boca Raton, FL 33487-2742

and by CRC Press
2 Park Square, Milton Park, Abingdon, Oxon, OX14 4RN

CRC Press is an imprint of Taylor & Francis Group, LLC

© 2023 Sufyan bin Uzayr

Library of Congress Cataloging-in-Publication Data

Names: Bin Uzayr, Sufyan, editor.
Title: Mastering KDE : a beginner's guide / edited by Sufyan bin Uzayr.
Description: First edition. | Boca Raton : CRC Press, 2023. | Series: Mastering computer science | Includes bibliographical references and index.
Identifiers: LCCN 2022021433 (print) | LCCN 2022021434 (ebook) |
ISBN 9781032313665 (hardback) | ISBN 9781032313658 (paperback) |
ISBN 9781003309406 (ebook)
Subjects: LCSH: KDE. | Linux. | Graphical user interfaces (Computer systems)
Classification: LCC QA76.9.U83 M38157 2023 (print) | LCC QA76.9.U83
(ebook) | DDC 005.4/37--dc23/eng/20220803
LC record available at https://lccn.loc.gov/2022021433
LC ebook record available at https://lccn.loc.gov/2022021434

ISBN: 9781032313665 (hbk)
ISBN: 9781032313658 (pbk)
ISBN: 9781003309406 (ebk)

DOI: 10.1201/9781003309406

Typeset in Minion
by KnowledgeWorks Global Ltd.

Contents

Preface

The *Mastering Computer Science* covers a wide range of topics, spanning programming languages as well as modern-day technologies and frameworks. The series has a special focus on beginner-level content, and is presented in an easy-to-understand manner, comprising:

- Crystal-clear text, spanning various topics sorted by relevance,

- A special focus on practical exercises, with numerous code samples and programs,

- A guided approach to programming, with step-by-step tutorials for the absolute beginners,

- Keen emphasis on real-world utility of skills, thereby cutting the redundant and seldom-used concepts and focusing instead of industry-prevalent coding paradigm, and

- A wide range of references and resources to help both beginner and intermediate-level developers gain the most out of the books.

The *Mastering Computer Science* series of books start from the core concepts, and then quickly move on to industry-standard coding practices, to help learners gain efficient and crucial skills in as little time as possible. The books assume no prior knowledge of coding, so even the absolute newbie coders can benefit from this series.

The *Mastering Computer Science* series is edited by Sufyan bin Uzayr, a writer and educator with more than a decade of experience in the computing field.

About the Author

Sufyan bin Uzayr is a writer, coder, and entrepreneur with over a decade of experience in the industry. He has authored several books in the past, pertaining to a diverse range of topics, ranging from History to Computers/IT.

Sufyan is the Director of Parakozm, a multinational IT company specializing in EdTech solutions. He also runs Zeba Academy, an online learning and teaching vertical with a focus on STEM fields.

Sufyan specializes in a wide variety of technologies such as JavaScript, Dart, WordPress, Drupal, Linux, and Python. He holds multiple degrees, including ones in Management, IT, Literature, and Political Science.

Sufyan is a digital nomad, dividing his time between four countries. He has lived and taught in universities and educational institutions around the globe. Sufyan takes a keen interest in technology, politics, literature, history, and sports, and in his spare time, he enjoys teaching coding and English to young students.

Learn more at sufyanism.com

CHAPTER 1

Introduction to KDE

IN THIS CHAPTER

> Ubuntu-based on GNU/Linux

> Open Source Linux desktop environment

> Applicable terms (GUI, CLI, TUI)

> KDE

> KDE-based Linux Distributions

> History of KDE

> KDE version list

> Features

> Advantages

In this introductory chapter, we will briefly discuss one of the best Linux-based operating systems named K(ool) Desktop Environment (KDE). Primarily, it is an official Linux OS and has various KDE features. KDE is based on the pure KDE built from the Ubuntu repositories. The first release was Beta 1 on October 20, 1997. Exactly one year after the original announcement. There are three additional Betas followed November 23, 1997, February 1, 1998, and April 19, 1998.

There are various terms to discuss to understand the concept of the Ubuntu KDE. So let's begin this with Ubuntu and then we move forward to the desktop environment KDE.

DOI: 10.1201/9781003309406-1

Now we are going to cover basic terms before going deep into the GNOME desktop environment such as GNU/Linux, Open Source, Free Software, GUI, TUI, CLI, and so on.

UBUNTU-BASED GNU/LINUX

Ubuntu is a "distribution" of GNU/Linux. Linux is the kernel layer. The software talks directly to the hardware: managing power, multitasking, and other low-level functions. Most Linux distributions include the GNU libraries and applications, including development tools, often referred to as GNU/Linux.

WHAT IS DISTRIBUTION?

The term "distribution" refers to the combination of these packaging of the Kernel with the GNU libraries and applications. Ubuntu is one such distribution. It contains the Linux kernel, the GNU tools, and many other applications and libraries.

OPEN SOURCE LINUX DESKTOP ENVIRONMENT

The word "Open Source" is the attribute to the Linux community, which brought it into existence along with the introduction of Linux. "Linux" came into existence as only a based on Kernel.

Many people and communities started contributing toward making it a complete operating system which could replace UNIX.

Free Software

"Free software" term is software that respects users' freedom and community. Approximately, it means that the users have the freedom to do anything such as run, copy, distribute, study, change, and improve the software. Therefore, "free software" is a topic of liberty, not price.

A program is a free software that adequately gives users all of these freedoms. Otherwise, it is nonfree.

Key Points:

- The freedom to run the program as per your wish

- Free software can be commercial

- The freedom to get the source code and make changes

- Legal considerations

- Contract-based licenses

Next, we will discuss the following terms, which are also related to the Ubuntu desktop environment GNOME. The times are GUI, CLI, and TUI. Useful terms are discussed in the following sections.

GUI (Graphical User Interface)

GNOME is the default GUI for most Ubuntu installations and is (loosely) based on the Apple ecosystem.

A GUI or graphical application is anything you can interact with using your mouse, touchpad, or touch screen. You have various icons and other visual prompts that you can activate with a mouse pointer to access the functionalities. DE provides the GUI to interact with your system. You can use GUI applications such as GIMP, VLC, Firefox, LibreOffice, and file manager for various tasks.

CLI (Command-Line Interface)

CLI is a command-line program that accepts inputs to perform a particular function. Any application you can use via commands in the terminal falls into this category.

TUI (Terminal User Interface)

TUI is also known as a Text-based User Interface.

You have text on the screen because they are used only in the terminal. These applications are not well known to many users, but there are a bunch of them. Terminal-based web browsers are an excellent example of TUI programs. Terminal-based games also fall into this category.

WHAT IS KDE?

KDE is a free software community that develops free, open source software. Still, as a central development hub, it provides you with various tools and resources that allow collaborative work on this software. Its well-known products include the Plasma Desktop (the default desktop environment on other various Linux distributions), KDE Frameworks with a range of cross-platform applications like Krita or digiKam applications to run on UNIX, UNIX-like desktops, Microsoft Windows, and Android.

K desktop environment is a desktop working platform with a GUI released in an open source package. When KDE was first released, it received a Kool desktop environment name, shortened as a K desktop environment. The KDE GUI is provided with everything users typically require, including a file manager, a window manager, a helpful tool, and a system configuration tool. The KDE project is still ongoing, and its developers discuss their collaborative plans online via an official KDE mailing list, newsgroups, and Internet relay chat.

Matthias Ettrich first launched the KDE project in 1996. He planned to offer a more suitable UNIX-based desktop environment for beginner computer users. He used a GUI, which is more understandable and straightforward for Windows OS users. KDE is currently employed with Linux, Solaris, FreeBSD, OpenBSD, and LinuxPPC.

Like LibreOffice in Ubuntu, KDE has KOffice considered a stylish suite among KDE applications. It includes a word processor and spreadsheet, image editing, vector drawing, and presentation applications. The application KOffice was first released in October 2000 as part of the KDE version 2.0 package.

HISTORY OF KDE

KDE was founded in 1996 by Matthias Ettrich, a student at the University of Tübingen, Germany.

At that time, he was troubled by various aspects of the UNIX desktop. His concern was that none of the applications looked or behaved alike. In his opinion, desktop applications were too complicated for end users. To solve the issue, he created a desktop environment in which users could expect the applications to be consistent and easy to use.

The name KDE was considered a wordplay on the existing Common Desktop Environment (CDE), available for UNIX systems. In contrast, CDE was an X11-based user environment developed by HP, IBM, and Sun through the X/Open consortium, an interface and productivity tool, which is based on the Motif graphical widget toolkit. It was like being an intuitively easy-to-use desktop computer environment. The K originally stood for "Kool," but it was quickly decided that the K should stand for nothing in particular. The KDE expanded to "K Desktop Environment" before it was dropped altogether instead of simply KDE in a rebranding effort.

In the beginning, Ettrich chose to use the Qt framework of Trolltech for the KDE project, but other programmers started developing KDE/Qt applications, and, by 1997, a few applications were being released. On July 12, 1998, the first version of the desktop environment, KDE 1.0, was released. The original GPL version of the toolkit only existed for platforms that used the X11 display server. Still, with Qt 4, LGPL licensed versions are available for more media. It allowed KDE software based on Qt 4 or newer versions to be distributed to Microsoft Windows and OS X theoretically.

The KDE team announced a rebranding of the KDE project on November 24, 2009. Inspired by the sensed shift in objectives, the rebranding focused on highlighting the community of software creators and the other tools supplied by the KDE rather than the desktop environment.

It was previously known as KDE 4, but now split into KDE Plasma Workspaces, Applications, and Platform bundled as KDE Software Compilation 4. Since 2014, the KDE now no longer stands for K Desktop Environment but the software's community.

What Is KDE Neon?

KDE Neon is a Linux distribution by KDE based on the Ubuntu long-term support (LTS) release, which was bundled with a set of additional software repositories containing the newest 64-bit versions of the Plasma 5 desktop environment, Plasma 5 framework, Qt 5 toolkit, and other compatible KDE software.

You can think of KDE as a GUI for Linux OS. KDE has proved Linux users to make its use as easy as they use windows. It provides Linux users a graphical interface to choose their customized desktop environment. You can select your graphical interface among various available GUI interfaces with their look.

You can imagine Linux without KDE and GNOME like DOS in windows. KDE and GNOME are similar to Windows, except they are related to Linux through x server rather than the operating system. When you install Linux, you choose your desktop environment from two or three different desktop environments like KDE and GNOME. Another popular environment, same as KDE, is GNOME. Both come with various features with other distributions. KDE comes with a variety of features. Some of the main among them are listed below:

- **Konqueror to browse files:** Same as Windows, KDE has a Konqueror, which is used to browse local files and can be used as a browser to browse the web.

- **KOffice software:** Like Microsoft office in windows, KDE comes with Kword, kpresenter, Kcalc, and Kontact. Moreover, KDE comes with an editor like KWrite, a default text editor of KDE, and is better than Notepad of Windows.

HISTORY OF RELEASES

First, we will discuss the software releases. There are five versions of KDE given below:

- K Desktop Environment 1
- K Desktop Environment 2
- K Desktop Environment 3
- KDE Software Compilation 4
- KDE Plasma 5

Let's discuss all the above versions in detail.

K Desktop Environment 1

Introduction

It was the initial series of releases of the K Desktop Environment. There are two major releases in this series. The development of KDE started right after Matthias Ettrich's announcement on October 14, 1996, 16 years ago (1996), to found the Kool Desktop Environment. The word Kool has dropped shortly afterward, and the name became simply K Desktop Environment.

In the beginning, every components were released to the developer community without any coordinated time frame throughout the overall project. The first communication of KDE via mailing list was called kde@fiwi02.wiwi.uni-Tubingen.de.

The initial release was Beta 1 on October 20, 1997, almost exactly one year after the original announcement. Three additional Betas followed November 23, 1997, February 1, 1998, and April 19, 1998.

K Desktop Environment 1.0

The initial version 1.0 of K Desktop Environments was released on July 12, 1998. KDE is a network transparent desktop environment for UNIX workstations. It seeks to fill the need for an easy-to-use desktop for UNIX workstations, similar to the desktop environments found under the MacOS or Windows. The UNIX operating system is the better operating system available today. UNIX has been the undisputed option of information technology for many years. When you look at stability, scalability, and openness, there is no competition to UNIX. However, the lack of an easy-to-use contemporary desktop environment for UNIX has prevented

UNIX from finding a way onto the desktops of the computer user in offices and homes. There is now an easy-to-use, contemporary desktop environment available for UNIX with KDE. With the implementation of UNIX, such as Linux, UNIX/KDE is an entirely free open computing platform available free of charge, including its source code to modify. We hope that the combination UNIX/KDE will finally bring open, reliable, stable, and monopoly-free computing to the average computer.

This version received a mixed reception that uses the Qt software framework under the Qt Free Edition License, which was claimed not to be compatible with free software, and advised the use of Motif or LessTif instead. Despite this, KDE was well received by many users and made its way into the first Linux distributions.

K Desktop Environment 1.1

K Desktop Environment 1.1 version was faster, more stable, and included many minor improvements. It had a new set of icons, backgrounds, and textures. Some components received more updates, such as the Konqueror predecessor kfm, the application launcher kpanel, and the KWin predecessor kwm. Then newly introduced, e.g., kab, a library for address management, and a rewrite of KMail, called kmail2, was installed as alpha in parallel to the classic KMail version. kmail2 never left the alpha state, and development was ended in updating classic KMail. K Desktop Environment 1.1 was well received among critics. At the same time, Trolltech prepared a 2.0 version of Qt, which was released as a beta on January 28, 1999. Consequently, no more extensive upgrades for KDE 1 based on Qt 1 were developed. Instead, only bug fixes were released: version 1.1.1 on May 3, 1999 and version 1.1.2 on September 13, 1999. A more profound upgrade and a port to Qt 2 were developed as K Desktop Environment 2.

Workspaces

Workspaces are used to reduce clutter and make the desktop easier to navigate. It also can be used to organize your work. For example, you could have communication windows, such as email and your chat program, on one workspace and your work on a different workspace. Workspaces used in K Desktop Environment 1.1 are given below:

1. KDM

2. KWin

3. Plasma

4. systemsettings

Let's discuss them in detail.

1. **KDM:** KDE Display Manager is a graphical user login interface for UNIX-like operating systems. The KDE SC 4 is a replacement for XDM, the default X display manager initially developed. KDM Display Manager allows users to pick their session type on a per-login basis. KDE SC uses the Qt toolkit and configures it from the System Settings. It also allows theming and user photos.

   A simple KDM login dialog box lists users on the left, stating username, their "real name," and also containing a small picture that the user or the administrator can choose. To the right from the list are a greeting and a photo. These items can be customized using System Settings. Users may also replace the picture with an analog clock. Under the clock are the Username and Password text boxes. On some systems, users can find a session selector under the password field to select the kind of session type they want to start, e.g., KDE, GNOME, or a simple terminal. A series of buttons offers commands to shut down and reboot your system, restart the X server, or start a tool to manage users.

2. **KWin:** It is a manager for the X Window System. It is an integral part of the KDE Software Compilation, although it can be used independently or with other desktop environments.

   There are various window decorations for KWin, including the default Oxygen, Microsoft Windows-like Redmond, and Keramik. IceWM themes can also be used, provided the kdeartwork package is installed. Currently available backends include XRender, OpenGL 1.x, OpenGL 2.x, and OpenGL ES 2.0. As of KDE 4.3, it has the following effects that are built-in:

   • **Accessibility:**

     – Name

     – Invert

     – Looking glass

     – Magnifier

- – Sharpen
- – Snap helper
- – Track mouse
- – Zoom
- **Appearance:**
  - – Explosion
  - – Fade
  - – Fade desktop
  - – Fall apart
  - – Highlight windows
  - – Login
  - – Logout
  - – Magic lamp
  - – Minimize animation
  - – Mouse mark
  - – Scale In
  - – Sheet
  - – Slide
  - – Sliding popups
  - – Taskbar thumbnails
  - – Thumbnail aside
  - – Translucency
  - – Wobbly windows
- **Window management:**
  - – Box switch
  - – Cover switch

- Desktop cube

- Desktop cube animation

- Desktop grid

- Flip switch

- Present windows

- Resize window

3. **KDE Plasma Workspaces:** Workspaces are the term for all graphical environments provided by KDE. Plasma separates components into "data engines" and visualization counterparts. It is intended to reduce the total programming effort when there are multiple possible visualizations of given data and make it easier for the data engine and the workspaces to be written independently. Currently, three workspaces are being developed:

- Plasma Desktop for traditional desktop PCs and notebooks

- Plasma Netbook for netbooks

- Plasma Active for tablet PCs and devices

There are various workspaces under the plasma.

- **Desktop:** Plasma Desktop is the first workspace that KDE developed. It was declared with the release of KDE SC 4.2. It is designed for desktop PCs and bigger laptops. The default configuration resembles K Desktop Environment 3 and Microsoft Windows XP, but extensive configurability allows radical departures from the default layout. It is a fundamental rewrite of several desktop interaction programs included in earlier K Desktop Environments for UNIX-like systems, focusing on eye candy and special graphical effects. The Desktop Workspace replaces the last KDesktop shell, Kicker taskbar, and SuperKaramba widget engine in the K Desktop Environment 3 with a unified widget system that can replace alternative designs.

- **Netbook:** Plasma Netbook is the second workspace. It aims at netbooks (Netbooks are a category of small, lightweight, legacy-free, and inexpensive laptop computers) and may also be used on tablet PCs – the first stable release shipped with KDE SC 4.4.

- **Plasma Active:** It is not a workspace on its own and a service built on top of the frameworks that enable the creation of full-fledged workspaces using only QML files without the need to program in C++. Plasma Active serves as the base for touchscreen-compatible workspaces. Active-compatible releases of the Kontact applications and a document viewer based on Calligra Suite are already available.

- **Contour:** Contour is the Plasma interface for tablet devices. Its development was initiated in April 2011 by basysKom. Replacing an earlier Tablet prototype, Contour is now the main workspace and was shipped as part of Plasma Active 1.0, released in October 2011.

- **Mobile:** The Plasma Mobile was targeted as smartphones and small tablet devices mainly used via touch input. It was initially released in 2011 along with Plasma Active 1.0, but the development focus shifted toward Contour. Plasma Mobile, meanwhile, has become part and has been superseded by Plasma Active.

Features:

- Plasma features essentially an applet that contains other applets. Two primary examples of containments are the desktop background and the taskbar. A containment is anything the developer wants: an image, animation, or even OpenGL. Images are commonly used, but with Plasma, the user could set any applet as the desktop background without losing the applet's functionality. This also allows applets to be dragged between the desktop and the taskbar and different visualization for the more confined taskbar. From KDE 4.0 to 4.2, the default theme such as Oxygen. It was characterized by dark tones. In KDE 4.3, the new Air theme is replaced, which predominates in transparency and white as the base color. New themes for Plasma can chose and installed through an authority.

- The Plasma widgets' scalability allows them to be resized and rotated to any size, with only a brief pause to redraw themselves. The Kross scripting framework will enable developers to write widgets in a variety of programming languages in addition to C++. Widgets are their size and can be made to show more or fewer data depending on their size.

- Plasma can support other widgets. SuperKaramba is the widget engine used in the KDE 3 series that has been added for legacy reasons.

Default environment: These operating systems offer it as the default environment:

- ALT Linux
- Ark Linux
- ArtistX
- aptosid
- BackTrack
- Chakra Linux
- Frugalware
- Kanotix
- Kororaa
- Kubuntu
- Mageia (DVD version)
- Mandriva Linux
- Magic Linux
- MCNLive
- MEPIS
- Netrunner (operating system)
- openSUSE
- Pardus
- PCLinuxOS
- Qomo Linux
- Sabayon Linux
- Slackware

- Skolelinux

- VectorLinux

- Z-Soft

- YOPER

- PC-BSD

- BeleniX

- SuperX

4. **System Settings:** It is a KDE application used to configure the system under KDE Plasma Workspaces. It replaces K Desktop Environment 3's KControl.

   Features:

   - Control Center for global KDE platform settings

   - All desktop settings converged on one central location

   - General and Advanced tabs separate most common user settings

   - The search function helps narrow down probable settings

K Desktop Environment 2

This was the second release of the K Desktop Environment (now called KDE Software Compilation). There were several major releases in this series.

Major updates:

1. K Desktop Environment 2 presented significant technical improvements compared to its predecessor.

2. Desktop COmmunication Protocol (DCOP) is a client-to-client communications protocol intermediated by a server over the standard X11 ICE library.

3. KIO, an application I/O library. It is network transparent that can access HTTP, FTP, POP, IMAP, NFS, SMB, LDAP, and local files. Moreover, it permits developers to "drop-in" other protocols, such as WebDAV, automatically available to all KDE applications. It can also locate handlers for particular MIME types.

4. These handlers can be embedded within the requesting application using the KParts technology.

5. KParts is a component object model that allows an application to embed another within itself. It handles all aspects of the embedding, such as positioning toolbars and inserting the proper menus when the component is activated. It can interface with the KIO to locate available handlers for specific MIME types or services/protocols.

6. KHTML, an HTML 4.0 obedient rendering and drawing engine. It supports many technologies such as JavaScript, Java, HTML 4.0, CSS 2, and SSL for secure communications. It is consistent with Netscape plugins such as Flash. KHTML also can embed components within itself using the KParts technology.

Following terms are used in the major updates.

DCOP

Desktop Communication Protocol (DCOP) was a lightweight interprocess and software componentry communication system. Its goal for the system was to allow applications to interoperate and share complex tasks. DCOP was a "remote control system that allowed applications or scripts to enlist the help of other applications. It was built on top of the X Window System Inter-Client Exchange protocol.

It provides extensive new capabilities without requiring entirely new applications to be written. KDE applications and the KDE libraries did make heavy use of DCOP, most of the KDE applications can control by scripts via the DCOP mechanism. D-Bus replaced DCOP in KDE Software Compilation 4. A command-line tool called "dcop" can be used for communication with the applications from the shell, where "kdcop" is a GUI tool to explore the interfaces of an application.

DCOP model   The model is simple. Each application using DCOP is a client. They communicate through a DCOP server, which functions like a traffic director, dispatching messages/calls to the proper destinations. All clients are peers of each other.

Two types of actions are likely with DCOP: "send and forget" messages, which do not block, and "calls," that block waiting for some data to be returned.

Any data sent is serialized (also referred to as marshaling in CORBA speak) using the built-in QDataStream operators available in all Qt classes. A simple IDL-like compiler is available, i.e., dcopidl and dcopidl2cpp that generates stubs and skeletons using the dcopidl compiler benefits safety. The Trinity Desktop Environment uses it.

X Window System

The X Window System, known as X11, is based on its current major version being 11 or shortened to simply X. Sometimes informally, X-Window is a computer software system and network protocol that provides a GUI and rich input device for networked computers. It creates an abstraction layer where software is written to use a generalized set of commands, allowing the reuse of programs on any computer that implements X.

X was originated at MIT (short for Massachusetts Institute of Technology) in 1984. Since September 1987, the protocol version has been X11. The X.Org Foundation conducts the X project, with the current reference implementation, X.Org Server, available as free and open source software under the MIT License and similar permissive licenses.

Purpose and Abilities of X Window System   X is an architecture system for remote GUIs and rich input device capabilities, allowing many people to share the power of a time sharing a computer and collaborate through client applications running on remote computers. Each person using a networked terminal can interact with the display with any user input device. X software on UNIX, Linux, and also Mac OS X is used to run client applications on computers when there is no need for time sharing.

X provides windowing on system displays and manages the keyboard, pointing device control functions, and touchscreens. Its standard distribution is a complete, albeit simple, display and interface solution that delivers a standard toolkit and protocol for GUI on UNIX operating systems and OpenVMS. It has been ported to many other contemporary general-purpose operating systems. The basic framework, or primitives, for building GUI environments like drawing and moving windows on. It also displays and interacts with a mouse, keyboard, or touchscreen and does not mandate that the user interface be present; individual client programs known as window managers handle this. The visual styling of X-based environments varies greatly with different programs may present different interfaces. X is built as an additional abstraction layer on the operating system kernel.

KIO

KIO (short for KDE Input/Output) is part of the KDE architecture. It provides access to files, websites, and other resources through a single consistent API. Applications, such as Konqueror, which are written using this framework, can operate on files stored on remote servers the same way they work on those stored locally, effectively making KDE network transparent. It allows a file browser like Konqueror to be both a highly versatile and powerful file manager and a web browser. KIO can support individual protocols (e.g., HTTP, FTP, SMB, SSH, FISH, SFTP, SVN, and TAR). The KDE help center app Khelp has a kioslaves section that lists the available protocols with a short description.

K Desktop Environment 2.0

Konqueror was introduced as a web browser, file manager, and document viewer. It used KHTML for displaying web pages.

K Desktop Environment 2.0 is also the initial release of the KOffice suite, consisting of a spreadsheet application such as KSpread, a vector drawing application such as KIllustrator, a frame-based word-processing application such as KWord, a presentation program such as KPresenter, and a chart and diagram application such as KChart. The native file formats were XML based. The KOffice suite included a scripting language that has the ability to embed individual components within each other using KParts.

Following are the terms used in the above lines.

Konqueror   It is a web browser and file manager that provides the file viewer functionality for systems such as files on a remote FTP server, as local files, and files in a disk image. It is developed by developers and can run on most UNIX-like operating and Windows systems. It is a center part of the KDE Software Compilation. It is licensed and distributed under the GNU General Public License version 2.

The name "Konqueror" referred to the two primary competitors when the Konqueror browser was the first release: "first comes the Navigator, Explorer, and then the Konqueror." It follows the KDE naming convention, and most KDE programs begin with the letter K.

It was released with version 2 on October 23, 2000. It replaces its predecessor, KFM which means KDE file manager. With the release of KDE4, Konqueror was replaced as the default file manager by Dolphin.

Major supported protocols:

- FTP and SFTP/SSH browser

- SAMBA (Microsoft file-sharing) browser

- HTTP browser

- IMAP mail client

- ISO (CD image) viewer

- VNC viewer

The User Interface of Konqueror   Konqueror's user interface of Microsoft's Internet Explorer is more customizable. It works well with "panels," which can rearrange or add. For example, an Internet bookmarks panel on the left side of the browser, and by clicking a bookmark, the respective web page will be viewed in the larger panel to the right. Other, a hierarchical list of folders in one panel and the content of the selected folder in another. Panels are pretty flexible and can even include, among other KParts, components, a console window, a text editor, a media player. The panel configurations can be saved, and there are some default configurations.

Navigation functions, such as the back, forward, history, etc., are available during all operations. Most of the keyboard shortcuts can remap using a graphical configuration, and navigation can be conducted by assigning letters to nodes on the active file by pressing the control key. The address bar has autocompletion support for local directories, past URLs, and past search terms.

The application uses a tabbed interface, wherein a window can contain multiple documents in tabs. Numerous document interfaces are not supported; however, it is possible to recursively divide a window to view multiple documents simultaneously or open another window.

Web Browser Konqueror   Konqueror has been developed as an independent web browser project. It uses KHTML as its layout engine, is compliant with HTML, and supports JavaScript, Java applets, CSS, SSL, and other relevant open standards. An alternative layout engine, kwebkitpart, is available from the Extragear.

While KHTML is the default web-rendering engine, Konqueror is a modular application, and other rendering engines have been available.

Especially the WebKitPart that uses the KHTML-derived WebKit engine has seen a lot of support in the KDE 4 series.

K Desktop Environment 2.1

The K Desktop Environment 2.1 released the media player noatun, which used a modular plugin design. For development, K Desktop Environment 2.1 was bundled with KDevelop.

K Desktop Environment 2.2

The KDE 2.2 release improved application startup time on GNU/Linux systems and increased HTML rendering and JavaScript stability and capabilities. Several new plugins were included in Konqueror. KMail received IMAP support, including SSL and TLS, while KOrganizer got native iCalendar support. Other improvements included a new plugin-based print architecture and a personalization wizard.

K Desktop Environment 3

It is the third series of releases of the K Desktop Environment, now called KDE Software Compilation. There are six major releases in the series.

K Desktop Environment 3.0

It introduced support for restricted usage, a feature demanded by specific environments such as kiosks, Internet cafes, and enterprise deployments, which disallows from having full access to all capabilities of a piece of software to preclude specific undesirable actions. KDE version 3.0 included a new lockdown framework to address these needs, mainly a permissions-based system for changing app configuration that supplements the basic UNIX permissions system. The KDE panel and the desktop manager were modified to employ the technique. Still, other major desktop components, such as Konqueror and the Control Center, had to wait for releases.

K Desktop Environment 3.0 has a new printing framework, KDEPrint. KDEPrint's modular design supported different printing engines, such as CUPS, LPRng, and LDP/LPR. In conjunction with CUPS, KDEPrint managed. Since KDEPrint provides a command-line interface framework, including GUI configuration elements, access to non-KDE applications, such as OpenOffice.org, the Mozilla Suite, and Acrobat Reader.

This release introduced a new KDE address book library with a central address book for all KDE applications. The library is based on the vCard standard and extended by additional backends such as LDAP and database servers.

K Desktop Environment 3.1

K Desktop Environment 3.1 with Konqueror and the About screen. Version 3.1 introduced a new default window (Keramik) and icon (Crystal) styles and several enhancements.

The update included greatly improved LDAP integration via Kontact enhanced security for KMail. Also support S/MIME, PGP/MIME, and X.509v3. Microsoft Exchange 2000 compatibility KOrganizer. The desktop framework introduced in version 3.0 was extended. Other improvements included:

- It used to tabbed browsing in Konqueror.

- KGet is a new download manager.

- A new multimedia plugin based on Xine and a desktop sharing framework.

K Desktop Environment 3.2

K Desktop Environment version 3.2 with Konqueror and the About screen. This release has been described for the K Desktop Environment.

K Desktop Environment version 3.2 included new features, such as spell checking for forms and emails, tabs in the Konqueror application, improved email support, also for Microsoft Windows desktop sharing protocol (RDP). Performance and Freedesktop.org standards compliance was improved by lower start-up times for applications and strengthened interoperability with other Linux and UNIX software. After the KDE community worked with Apple's Safari web browser team, KDE's web support performance boosts and increased compliance with web standards.

K Desktop Environment improved usability by many applications, dialogs, control panels to focus on clarity, utility, and reducing clutter in various menus and toolbars. There are hundreds of new icons are created to improve the consistency of the environment, with changes to the default visual style, including new screens, animated progress bars, and styled panels. The Plastik style debuted in this release.

New applications included:

JukeBox   It was started by Scott Wheeler in 2000 and was initially called QTagger and was the first official part of KDE in KDE 3.2. JuK is a juke-box-style music player. It is a free software audio player by KDE, the default player since K Desktop Environment 3.2, and supports collections of MP3, Ogg Vorbis, and FLAC audio files. It is primarily an audio jukebox application with a strong focus on music management.
The following features:

- Collection list and multiple user-defined playlists.

- It can scan directories to automatically import playlists (.m3u files) and music files on startup.

- Dynamic Search Playlists can be automatically updated as fields in the collection change.

- It has tree View mode, where playlists automatically record albums, artists, and genres.

- It has a playlist history to indicate which files have been played and when.

- Support inline search for filtering the list of visible items.

- It can guess tag information from the file name.

- File renamer can rename files based on the tag content.

- Support ID3v1, ID3v2, and Ogg Vorbis tag reading and editing (via TagLib).

Kopete   It is a multi-protocol and free software instant messaging client released in the KDE Software Compilation. However, it can run in multiple environments, it was designed and integrated with the KDE Plasma Workspaces. The designated successor is KDE Telepathy from the KDE RTCC Initiative.
Features:

- It allows for grouping messages within a window, with tabs for easy switching of conversations.

- It can use multiple accounts on multiple services.

- Alias nicknames for contacts.

- It allows contact grouping.

- Custom notifications for contacts.

- KAddressBook and KMail integration.

- Conversation logging.

- It has custom emoticons.

- Custom notifications, including popups and sounds.

- QQ and Yahoo! messenger webcam support.

- On the fly spell checking.

- Voice calls via GoogleTalk and Skype.

KWallet   It (short for KDE Wallet Manager) is a credentials management application for the KDE Software Compilation desktop environment. It provides a way to store sensitive passwords in encrypted files, called "wallets." For added security, each wallet can be used to store different kinds of credentials, each with its password.

Kontact   It is an information manager and groupware software suite developed by KDE. It supports contacts, calendars, notes, to-do lists, news, and email. It offers several inter-changeable graphical UIs, such as KMail, KAddressBook, Akregator, etc., built on top of a common core.
    Other:

- KIG, an interactive geometry program.

- KSVG, an SVG viewer.

- KMag, KMouseTool, and KMouth are new accessibility tools.

- KGoldRunner, a new game.

K Desktop Environment 3.3
K Desktop Environment version 3.3 focused on different desktop components. Kontact was combined with Kolab, a groupware application, and Kpilot. Konqueror is given better support for instant messaging contacts, can send files to IM contacts, and supports IM protocols. KMail has given

the ability to display the online presence of IM contacts. Juk supports for burning audio CDs with K3b.

This update also included many minor desktop enhancements. Konqueror application received tab improvements, an RSS feed viewer sidebar, and a search bar compatible with all keyword searches. KMail was given HTML composition, anti-spam, anti-virus wizards, automatic handling of mailing lists, support for cryptography, and a quick search bar. Kopete support for file transfers with Jabber, aRts gained jack support, and KWin achieved new buttons to support more features.

New applications included:

- Kolourpaint is a KPaint replacement.

- KWordQuiz, KLatin, and KTurtle are education packages for schools and families.

- Kimagemapeditor and klinkstatus tools for web designers.

- KSpell2, a new spellchecking library, is improving on KSpell's shortcomings.

- KThemeManager is a new control center module for the global handling of KDE visual themes.

K Desktop Environment 3.4

K Desktop Environment version 3.4 focused on improving accessibility. The update added a text-to-speech system supporting Konqueror, Kate, KPDF, the standalone application KSayIt, and text-to-speech synthesis on the desktop. A high-contrast style, a complete monochrome icon set was added, and an icon effect of painting all KDE icons into any two arbitrary colors.

Kontact support for various groupware servers, whereas Kopete was integrated into Kontact. KMail can store passwords securely in KWallet. KPDF can select, copy, and paste text and images from PDFs, along with other improvements. The latest update added a new application, Akregator, which can read news from various RSS-enabled websites all in one application.

The latest update added DBUS/HAL support to allow dynamic device icons to keep in sync with the state of all devices. The kicker has improved visual aesthetic, and the trash system was redesigned to be more flexible. The new desktop allows SVG to be used as wallpapers. KHTML was enhanced standards support, having nearly complete support for CSS 2.1 and CSS 3. KHTML plugins are allowed to be activated on a case-by-case basis. There are also improvements to the way Netscape plugins are handled.

K Desktop Environment 3.5

The K Desktop Environment 3.5 has SuperKaramba, which provides integrated and simple-to-install widgets to the desktop. Konqueror's ad-block feature made the second web browser pass the Acid2 CSS test, ahead of Firefox and Internet Explorer. Kopete application gained webcam support for the MSN and Yahoo! IM protocols. The edutainment module has three new applications, KGeography, Kanagram, and blinKen. Kalzium also saw improvements.

THE TRINITY DESKTOP ENVIRONMENT

The Trinity Desktop Environment project, organized and led by Timothy Pearson, Kubuntu release manager for KDE 3.5, has released Trinity to pick up where the KDE e.V. left. This keeps the KDE 3.5 branch alive and releases bugs fixes, additional features, and compatibility with recent hardware. Trinity is packaged for Debian, Ubuntu, Red Hat, and other distributions.

The Kolab Enterprise packages are still being developed and tested on Kontact 3.5. A version based on Kontact 4 is available but not yet recommended for regular use.

KDE Software Compilation 4 (KDE SC 4)

KDE Software Compilation 4 is the current series of releases of KDE Software Compilation. The first major version (4.0) of the series was released on January 11, 2008, and the latest major version (4.10) was released on February 6, 2013. Whereas major releases (4. x) come within six months, minor bugfix releases (4.x.y) come monthly.

The new series includes several of the KDE Platform components, which contain an API called Phonon with framework Solid having default icon called as Oxygen. It has a new unique desktop and panel user interface called Plasma, which supports desktop widgets, replacing K Desktop Environment 3's separate components.

KDE Platform 4 makes it easy for KDE applications to be portable to different operating systems and made possible by the port to Qt version 4, which support non-X11-based platforms having Microsoft Windows and Mac OS X. Versions 4.0–4.3 of the KDE Compilation are known simply as

KDE 4. The change was a component of the KDE project's rebranding to reflect its increased scope.

Released Versions of KDE 4

KDE 4.0

Most development is implemented in most of the new technologies and frameworks of KDE 4. Both Plasma and the Oxygen style are two of the most significant user-facing changes.

Now, Dolphin replaces Konqueror as the default file manager in KDE 4.0. It addresses complaints of Konqueror being complicated for a simple file manager. However, Dolphin and Konqueror share as much code as possible, and Dolphin can embed it in Konqueror to allow Konqueror to be still used as a file manager.

Okular replaces other document viewers used in KDE 3 like KPDF, KGhostView, and KDVI. It uses software libraries and can be extended to view almost any document. Like Konqueror and KPDF in KDE version 3, Okular can also be embedded in other applications.

Release

On January 11, 2008, KDE 4 was released. Despite being labeled a stable release, it was intended for early adopters. Using KDE 3.5 was suggested for users wanting a more stable, "feature complete" desktop.

The release of KDE 4.0 met with a mixed reception. While early adopters tolerated the lack of finish for some of its new features, the release was widely criticized for its lack of stability and its "beta" quality.

Computerworld reporter Steven Vaugh an-Nichols criticized KDE 4.0 and 4.1 and called for a fork of KDE 3.5 by rebuild it on top of Qt 4. The same reporter praised KDE 4.3 and welcomed Trinity's KDE 3.5 continuation project. However, Linus Torvalds switched from GNOME to KDE in December 2005; GNOME after Fedora replaced KDE 3.5 with 4.0. In an interview with Computer world, he described KDE 4.0 as a "break everything" model and "half-baked" release, claiming that he expected it to be an upgrade of KDE version 3.5 was that there were significant cases of features being regressed due to its extensive changes.

Major updates of KDE 4

Many applications such as Extragear and KOffice modules have acquired numerous improvements with the new features of KDE 4 and Qt 4. But since they follow their release schedule, they were not available at the time of the first KDE 4 release these include application such as Amarok, K3b, digiKam, KWord, and Krita.

The Qt 4 series enabled KDE 4 to use less memory and be noticeably faster than KDE 3. The KDE libraries have been made more efficient. However, KDE 4.4 has the highest memory utilization on default Ubuntu installations compared to GNOME 2.29, Xfce 4.6. The version LXDE 0.5. Qt version 4 is available under the LGPL for operating system Mac OS X & Windows which allowing KDE 4 to run on those platforms. On August 2010, KDE Software compilation four on Mac OS X is considered as beta, while on Windows is not in the final state, so applications can be unsuitable for day-to-day use yet. Both ports try to use as little divergent code as possible to make the applications function almost identically on all platforms. During Summer of Code 2007, an icon cache was created to decrease application start-up times in KDE 4. Improvements were varied – Kfind, an application that used several hundred icons. Other applications and an entire KDE session started a little over a second faster.

Pre-releases

KDE 4.0 Alpha 1 was released in the market after adding significant features to KDE base libraries and shifting the focus onto integrating the new technologies into applications and the primary desktop. Alpha 1 had new frameworks to build applications with, providing improved hardware and multimedia integration through Solid and Phonon. Dolphin and Okular were integrated, and a unique visual appearance was provided through Oxygen icons.

Alpha 2 was released mainly focused on integrating the Plasma Desktop, improving the functionality, and stabilizing KDE.

Beta 1 was released with significant features included a pixmap cache – speeding up icon loading, KDE PIM improvements, improved KWin effects and configuration, better interaction between Konqueror and Dolphin, and Metalink support added KGet for enhanced downloads.

Beta 2 was released with the support of BSD and Solaris. The release included:

- The addition of the Blitz graphic library.

- Allowing developers to use high-performance graphical tricks like icon animation.

- KRDC (K Remote Desktop Client) overhaul for Google's Summer of Code.

- Plasma provides Amarok's central context view.

Beta 3 was released to focus on stabilizing and finishing the design of libraries for the release of the KDE Development Platform. Plasma had many new features, including an applet browser. The educational software received many improvements like Marble and Parley with bug fixes in other applications.

Beta 4 was released. A list of release blockers was compiled, listing issues that need to be resolved before KDE starts with the desktop's release candidate cycle. The goal is to focus on stabilization and fixing the release blockers.

At the same time, the first release of the KDE 4.0 Development Platform was released containing all the base libraries to develop KDE applications, including "widget libraries, a network abstraction layer and various libraries for multimedia integration, hardware integration and transparent access to resources on the network."

Let's discuss the version of KDE 4.0.

KDE 4.1

It was released on July 29, 2008, and included a shared emoticon theming system used in PIM, Kopete, and DXS, which lets applications download and install data from the Internet with one click. Also introduced are GStreamer application, QuickTime 7, and DirectShow 9 Phonon backends. Plasma improvements support Qt 4 widgets and WebKit integration, allowing many Apple Dashboard widgets to be displayed. There are also ports of some applications to Windows and Mac OS X.

New applications include:

- Dragon Player multimedia player (formerly Codeine)

- Kontact with some Akonadi functionality

- Skanlite is a scanner application

- Step physics is a simulator

- Games – Kdiamond Kollision, Kubrick, KsirK, and KBreakout

KDE 4.2

KDE 4.2 shows KMail, Dolphin, and was released on January 27, 2009. The release is viewed as a significant improvement beyond KDE 4.1 in nearly all aspects and a suitable replacement for KDE 3.5 for most users.

KDE Workspace improvements

The 4.2 release includes the number of bug fixes that have implemented many features present in KDE 3.5 but had been missing in KDE 4.0 and 4.1. These include multiple row layout and grouping in the taskbar, icon hiding in the system tray, panel autohiding, window previews, and tooltips are back in the panel and taskbar, notifications, job tracking by Plasma, and have icons on the desktop using a Folder View as the desktop background where icons remain where they are placed.

New Plasma includes leaving messages on a locked screen, previewing files, switching desktop activities, monitoring news feeds, and utilities like the Pastebin applet, the calendar, timer, unique character selector, a QuickLaunch widget, and a system monitor, among many others. The Plasma workspace can load Google Gadgets. Its widgets can be written in Ruby and Python also, support for applets written in JavaScript and Mac OS X dashboard widgets has been improved.

New desktop alterations have been added, such as the Magic Lamp, Minimize impact, and the Cube and Sphere desktop switchers. Others, such as the desktop grid, have been improved. The user interface for choosing effects has been reworked to select the most commonly used results easily. Compositing desktop effects have been enabled by default where hardware and drivers support them. Automatic checks confirm that compositing works before allowing it on the workspace.

KRunner – the "Run command..." dialog – has extended functionality through several new plugins, including spellchecking, Konqueror browser history, power management control through PowerDevil, KDE Places, Recent Documents, and the ability to start specific sessions of the Kate editor, Konqueror, and Konsole. The converter plugin also supports quickly converting between speed, mass, and distance units.

Multi-screen support has been improved via the Kephal library by fixing multiple bugs when running KDE on more than one monitor.

KDE 4.3

KDE 4.3 desktop was released on August 4, 2009, showing Dolphin, KMail, and a selection of desktop widgets, with this release being described as incremental and lacking in significant new features. It fixed over 10,000 bugs and implemented almost 2,000 feature requests. Also, integration with other technologies, such as PolicyKit, NetworkManager, and Geolocation services, was another focus of this release. A more flexible system tray has developed many new Plasmoids including the openDesktop.

org Plasmoid, a first take on the Social Desktop. Plasma also receives more keyboard shortcuts.

KDE SC 4.4

It was released on February 9, 2010, based on version 4.6 of the Qt 4 toolkit. As such, KDE SC 4.4 carries Qt's performance improvements and Qt 4.6's new features, such as the new animation framework Kinetic. A completely new application replaces KAddressBook with the same name – previously tentatively called KContactManager. The new KAddressBook is Akonadi integration and has a streamlined user interface. Another significant new feature is an additional new Plasma interface targeted toward netbooks. Kopete is released as version 1.0. KAuth, a cross-platform authentication API, made its début in KDE SC 4.4. Initially, only PolicyKit is supported as a backend.

KDE SC 4.5

KDE SC 4.5 was released on August 10, 2010. New features include integrating the WebKit library, an open source web browser engine used in major browsers such as Apple Safari and Google Chrome. KDE's KHTML engine will continue to be developed, whereas KPackage has been deprecated, and KPackageKit was suggested to replace it, but it didn't make it replace it.

KDE SC 4.6

KDE SC 4.6 was released on January 26, 2011, and had better OpenGL compositing along with the usual myriad of fixes and features.

KDE SC 4.7

It was released on July 28, 2011. The version updated KWin to be compatible with OpenGL ES 2.0, which will enhance its portability to mobile and tablet platforms. Other optimizations, such as Qt Quick, were made to strengthen this portability. This version brought some updates and enhancements to Plasma Desktop, such as better network management and updates to certain widgets and activities.

Apart from the desktop environment, version 4.7 updates many applications within the Software Compilation. The Dolphin file manager has been updated to provide a clean user interface. Now it supports voice navigation, map creation, and new plugins. The Gwenview image viewer allows users to compare more than two photos side by side. The Kontact database has been ported to Akonadi, allowing the database to be accessible from other applications.

DigiKam has been supporting face detection, image versioning, and image tagging. Other applications, such as Kate, Kalzium, KAlgebra, KStars, and KDevelop, have been updated. Moreover, version 4.7 fixed over 12,000 bugs.

KDE SC 4.8

KDE SC Release 4.8 was available on January 25, 2012.

Plasma Workspaces

KWin performance was increased by optimizing effect rendering. Window resizing was improved as well. Other KWin are QML-based Window switcher, initial Wayland support and AnimationEffect class.

Applications

A new version of Dolphin shipped with KDE applications 4.8. It has improved performance with better file animated transitions, name display with other new and improved features.

KDE SC 4.9

KDE SC 4.9 was available on August 1, 2012. The release featured various improvements to the Dolphin file manager, including the reintroduction of in-line file renaming, back and forward mouse buttons, the advance of the places panel, and better usage of file metadata. More, there were several improvements to KWin and Konsole. Activities were better integrated with the workspace – several updated applications, including Okular, Kopete, Kontact, and educational applications.

KDE SC 4.10

It was released on February 6, 2013. Many default Plasma widgets were rewritten in QML, and Nepomuk, Kontact, and Okular improved significantly.

KDE SC 4.11

KDE SC 4.11 was released on August 14, 2013. Kontact and Nepomuk received many optimizations. The first generation Plasma Workspaces entered maintenance-only development mode.

KDE SC 4.12

KDE SC 4.12 was launched on December 18, 2013. The Kontact received substantial improvements.

KDE SC 4.13

KDE SC 4.13 was released on April 16, 2014. The Nepomuk semantic desktop search was replaced with KDE's in-house Baloo. KDE SC 4.13 was released in 53 different translations.

KDE SC 4.14

KDE SC 4.14 was launched on August 20, 2014. The release primarily focused on stability, with numerous bugs fixed and a few new features added. This was the final KDE SC 4 release.

KDE Plasma 5

It is the fifth and current generation of the visual workspaces environment created by KDE, mainly for Linux systems. KDE Plasma version 5 is the successor of KDE Plasma 4 and was released on July 15, 2014.

It includes a new theme, known as "Breeze," and increased convergence across different devices. The graphical interface was migrated to QML, which uses OpenGL for hardware acceleration, which resulted in better performance and reduced power consumption. Its Mobile is a Plasma 5 variant for Linux-based smartphones.

Software Architecture

KDE Plasma version 5 is built using Qt 5 and KDE Frameworks 5. It improves support for HiDPI displays and a convertible graphical shell, adjusting. KDE 5.0 also includes a new default theme. Qt 5's QtQuick 2 uses a hardware-accelerated OpenGL scene graph to compose and render graphics on the screen, allowing the offloading of computationally expensive graphics rendering tasks onto the GPU, freeing up resources on the system's main CPU.

KDE Plasma 5

It uses the X Window System. It supports that Wayland was prepared in the compositor and planned for a later release. It was created initially available in the 5.4 release. Stable support for an introductory Wayland session was provided in the 5.5 release (December 2015).

Support for NVIDIA proprietary driver for Plasma on Wayland was added in the 5.16 release (June 2019).

Development

Since the KDE Software Compilations split into KDE Plasma, KDE Frameworks, and KDE applications, each subproject can develop at its own pace. KDE Plasma 5 is on its release schedule, with feature releases every four months and bugfix releases in the intervening months.

Workspaces

The latest Plasma 5 features the following workspaces:

- Plasma Desktop for any mouse or keyboard driven computing devices like desktops or laptops.

- Plasma Mobile for smartphones.

- Plasma Bigscreen for TVs and set-top boxes including voice interaction.

- Plasma Nano, a minimal shell for embedded and touch-enabled devices, like IoT or automotive.

Desktop Features

- KRunner is a search feature with many available plugins. In addition to launching apps, can find files and folders, open websites, convert from one currency to another, calculate simple mathematical expressions, and perform numerous other valuable tasks.

- Flexible desktop and panel layouts composed of Widgets, also known as "Plasmoids," can be configured, moved around, replaced with alternatives, or deleted. Each screen layout can be individually configured. New widgets created can be downloaded within Plasma.

- Have a powerful clipboard with a memory of pieces of text that can call up at will.

- Systemwide notification system supporting fast reply, drag-and-drop straight from notifications, history view, and a Do Not Disturb mode.

- Central location to control media playback in open apps, your phone, or your web browser.

- Activities allow you to separate methods of using the system into distinct workspaces. Each activity can have a set of favorite and recently used applications, wallpapers, "virtual desktops," panels, window styles, and layout configurations. It also couples with ksmserver (i.e., X Session Manager implementation), which keeps track of apps that can be run or shut down along with given activity via subSessions functionality that keeps track of applications (not all applications support this feature as they don't implement XSMP protocol).

- Encrypted vaults for storing sensitive data.

- Night Color can automatically warm the screen colors at night, user-specified times, or manually.

- Style icons, cursors, application colors, user interface elements, splash screens, and more can change. Global Themes allow the entire look of the system to be modified in one click.

- Session Management allows apps running when the system shuts down to be automatically restarted in the same state they were in before.

Linux Distributions Using Plasma

Plasma 5 is a default desktop environment on Linux distributions, such as:

- ArcoLinux

- Fedora – KDE Plasma Desktop Edition is an official Fedora spin distributed by the project

- KaOS

- KDE Neon

- Kubuntu

- LliureX

- Manjaro – as Manjaro KDE edition

- MX Linux

- Netrunner

- openSUSE

- PCLinuxOS

- Q4OS

- Slackware

- Solus Plasma

- SteamOS 3.0

- Ubuntu Studio

History

The first Technology Preview of Plasma 5 was released on December 13, 2013. The first release version was on July 15, 2014, i.e., Plasma 5.0 saw the light of day. In 2015, Plasma 5 replaced Plasma 4 in many popular distributions, such as Fedora 22, Kubuntu 15.04, and openSUSE Tumbleweed.

Releases

Feature releases are released every four months and bugfix releases in the intervening months. Following version 5.8 LTS, KDE plans to support each new LTS version for 18 months with bug fixes, while new regular releases will see feature improvements.

LINUX DISTRIBUTIONS WITH KDE

KDE is one of the most useful and fastest desktop environments out in the market. While you can install KDE if you know-how, it is best to choose a Linux distribution that comes with KDE out-of-the-box.

Here is a complete list of some of the best KDE-based Linux distros:

1. KDE Neon

2. Kubuntu

3. Manjaro KDE

4. Fedora KDE Spin

5. openSUSE

6. Garuda Linux

7. Nitrux OS

8. MX Linux KDE

9. Alt Workstation K

10. ROSA

More Information about GNOME-Based Linux Distributions

KDE is a community. Plasma (i.e., previously K Desktop Environment) is a DE. Kubuntu is an Ubuntu with KDE Plasma. KDE Neon is a project (assume Linux distribution). It's similar to Kubuntu, but all KDE applications are in their latest version.

In other words, KDE is a group whose desktop environment is Plasma (Previously KDE Desktop). KDE Neon is Ubuntu LTE-based Linux + Plasma Desktop released by KDE itself. Kubuntu is Ubuntu + Plasma Desktop.

KDE Neon

KDE Neon is an updated software repository where most users want to use the packages built from released software that make up the User Edition. KDE contributors can use the packages built from KDE Git in the Testing and Unstable Editions. It uses the foundation of the newest Ubuntu LTS (20.04).

KDE Neon is a Linux distribution by KDE based on the latest Ubuntu LTS release, with several additional repositories containing the latest 64-bit versions of the Plasma 5 desktop environment with framework Qt 5 toolkit and other compatible KDE software. The first announcement was made in June 2016 by Kubuntu founder Jonathan Riddell following his departure from Canonical (Ubuntu's company). Ubuntu's official KDE Plasma-focused distribution targets the exact user as Kubuntu and differs primarily in a much shorter timeframe for users to receive updated Qt and KDE software. It is available in four release channels: User, Test, Unstable, and Developer Editions.

The KDE Neon Linux distribution mainly focused on the development of KDE. The emphasis is on cutting-edge software packages directly from KDE, giving programmers early access to new features but potentially at the expense of greater susceptibility to software bugs.

KDE Neon is confused with Kubuntu and vice versa, as Kubuntu has the KDE Plasma package on an Ubuntu-based operating system. However, the main difference between the two operating systems is that Kubuntu maintains stable releases and the LTS version of Ubuntu. At the same time, KDE Neon focuses on updating developer versions of KDE applications without supporting stable releases unless Ubuntu root users actively choose to upgrade systems.

Differentiates between KDE Neon and KDE Plasma

KDE Neon only allows the latest KDE applications to run on it. KDE Neon is explicitly made for KDE users, as it only accepts KDE applications and cannot run non-KDE programs. The feature regularly receives updates and is the first to experience newly-developed KDE applications. Since it also employs Plasma as its default desktop environment, Neon is exceptionally lightweight. It has a beautiful visual appearance, boosted by eye-catching icons, mesmerizing animations, and polished widgets.

Since both Neon and Plasma are based on and developed by KDE, they are similar and bear a striking resemblance to Windows. However, prefer using lighter themes and has shorter icons in the bottom panel. On the other hand, Plasma prefers a more vanilla KDE flavor, having more spread-out panels. It is similar in appearance to Windows XP.

KDE Neon regularly updates all the KDE applications, even the newly developed ones. If a new release for KDE comes out, KDE Neon will continue to feature support and allow users to install the latest versions. Plasma users continue to be stuck with the older version. However, this can be somewhat resolved by using the non-stable version of the applications.

Both Plasma and Neon are the products of KDE. Therefore, both use the Discover Software Center, though Plasma has more limitations to its software availability. In addition to the Discover Software Center, Neon has more options and supports for other package managers such as Flatpak.

openSUSE

It originates from the original SUSE Linux distribution and a community-based distribution in contrast to SUSE Linux Enterprise. The SUSE company is still an influential sponsor of openSUSE. The relationship is similar to Fedora, CentOS, to Red Hat Enterprise Linux. The project uses a gecko logo to show the relationship between SUSE and openSUSE.

It is available in two flavors, the rolling-release Tumbleweed the stable Leap. The latter is the same as Arch Linux as it is more of a "bleeding-edge" distribution with new software. You can install openSUSE as an old Linux system, but it is also available in the Windows Store for WSL. It may be neglected compared to other major Linux distributions, but it has a unique set of features and a codebase with a wealthy estate.

openSUSE also gives you access to vanilla GNOME. But unlike Fedora, it follows a much slower release schedule. You won't get access to all the latest GNOME features as soon as they are released. However, this isn't technically a bad thing. It can dedicate more time and effort to make the OS more stable and reliable by having a slow release cycle. It makes a perfect fit for professionals who can't afford to have their system crash in the middle of meaningful work. Now, openSUSE is distributed under two release models – Leap and Tumbleweed.

Each major version is released every three years, whereas point releases or minor updates are released annually with Leap. Depending on how often you want to upgrade your system, you should pick the flavor.

The openSUSE project offers the following two distributions:

- Tumbleweed, which is a rolling distribution.

- Leap, which is a point distribution.

What is openSUSE used for?

It is a project that promotes the benefit of free and open source software. Linux distributions are well known, mainly Tumbleweed, a tested rolling release, and Leap, a distribution with LTS.

However, starting and switching applications work differently from other desktop operating systems. It only uses a single panel at the top of the screen. Its session is started on Wayland.

Obtain KDE Software on openSUSE

KDE Software is preselected on installations from the openSUSE DVD, so click via the installation. If you like to save download time, burn the Live KDE image to a CD or a USB stick. Now, all the same, software is available online via YaST Software Management.

Plasma Desktop by KDE is the default workspace on openSUSE DE. It offers an elegant working environment that carries the full advantage of your system capabilities and the latest technology developments to support you in working or playing. It combines the power of Qt with KDE's high-resolution, the leading toolkit, artwork, clean, discreet themes, powerful widgets, WebKit for online content, and user experience effects into a consistent desktop that can shape in nearly limitless ways. The configuration provides a conventional desktop, whereas Plasma Desktop's flexible design gives the power to intuitively arrange panels, menus, icons, and widgets.

The KDE Platform has provided a wide range of applications since the beginning of the KDE project in 1996. These KDE applications are easy to learn due to a consistent look and feel and familiar design across applications and also are fast and reliable by a high degree of integration and sharing of all components with each other and the workspace.

KDE Plasma basics in openSUSE

KDE is a technology team that creates free and open source software for desktop and portable computing. Plasma, made by KDE, is the default graphical desktop environment of openSUSE. The latest version, Plasma 5, is a fresh, elegant, and powerful desktop for beginners and advanced users.

KDE software is not limited to single desktop environment. The software made by the community includes:

- Plasma is the graphical desktop.

- KDE applications are the collection of various applications for communication, work, education, and entertainment, including famous programs like Kate.

- Additional such as digiKam and Krit are high-quality applications.

- KDE Frameworks are the series of modules to quickly build new applications upon.

Things make KDE software on openSUSE special:

- It has a team of engineers who spend much of their time fixing bugs so that you can rely on KDE.

- It has a large, active community team that brings multiple points of view and different interests to the project.

- KDE software on openSUSE Distribution meets many users' needs.

- It stimulates the openSUSE distros to develop, evolve and progress.

These are the tools recommended by openSUSE for daily tasks:

1. **Firefox Browser with KDE Integration:** It offers a popular browser and improvements such as the KDE dialog for uploading or saving content, matching theming, and bookmarks.

2. **LibreOffice with KDE Integration:** It makes LibreOffice, the widely used office suite, fit right in with desktop.

3. Dolphin File Manager gives fast and powerful file management features for any content, whether it's hard disk, a memory stick, or a remote system.

4. **Okular Document Reader:** It is a broad file format support ensures that anyone can read whatever is on the computer because of its lightning startup time and support for advanced features such as PDF forms and highlighting.

5. **DigiKam Photo Management:** The powerful photo manager on Linux makes it easy to share shots on photography and social networking sites like Facebook, PicasaWeb SmugMug, etc. Prolific snappers can track thousands of shots with its powerful tagging with wide range of ways to search for images and appreciate its performance when viewing thumbnails or editing images. High-end photographers recognize its strong support for many RAW formats and high-bit depth editing.

6. **Choqok and Blogilo Application:** It lets you broadcast thoughts to the Twitter and Identi.ca microblogging networks, for the serious blogger, Blogilo eases writer for WordPress Blogspot, and many other sites.

7. **Music and Movies with Amarok and Kaffeine:** It manages the most significant music collections efficiently, lets user watch the video in the YouTube widget, shows you helpful information about artists, and enables you to discover acts using Web integration features, whereas Kaffeine is the lightweight way to watch movies and digital terrestrial TV.

8. **Kontact Personal Information Manager:** It helps stay on top of the email, schedule, and contacts in the office or at home.

9. Kopete Instant Messenger allows connection to all the popular Instant Messaging networks, including Facebook Chat, via the open XMPP protocol.

KDE Projects

The KDE community carries multiple free-software projects. The project formerly refers as KDE or KDE SC (Software Compilation), nowadays consists of three parts:

- **KDE Plasma:** It is a graphical desktop environment with customizable layouts and panels supporting virtual desktops and widgets. They are written with Qt 5 and KDE Frameworks 5.

- **KDE Frameworks:** It collects libraries and software frameworks built on Qt, formerly known as "kdelibs" or "KDE Platform."

- **KDE Applications:** Its utility applications (like Kdenlive or Krita) are mostly built on KDE Frameworks and are often part of the official KDE applications release.

KDE Plasma 5

KDE Plasma 5 is the fifth and present generation of the graphical workspaces environment created by KDE mainly for Linux systems. KDE Plasma version 5 is the successor of KDE Plasma 4.

It includes a default theme, known as "Breeze," and increased convergence across different devices. The interface was migrated to QML, which uses OpenGL for hardware acceleration, which resulted in better performance and reduced power consumption. Plasma Mobile is a KDE Plasma 5 variant for Linux-based smartphones.

Software architecture

Plasma 5 is built using Qt 5 and KDE Frameworks 5, mainly plasmaframework. It supports HiDPI displays and ships a graphical shell adjusting. It also includes a new default theme that is dubbed Breeze. QtQuick 2 uses a hardware-accelerated OpenGL(ES) scene graph (canvas) to compose and render graphics on the screen, allowing the offloading of expensive graphics rendering tasks onto the GPU freeing up resources on the system's main CPU.

Windowing systems

- It is running under Wayland.

- It uses the X Window System. Its support for Wayland was prepared in the compositor. It was made initially available in the 5.4 release. Its help in the Wayland session was provided in the 5.5 release.

- The NVIDIA proprietary driver for Plasma on Wayland was added in the 5.16 release (June 2019).

Workspaces

The Plasma 5 features the following workspaces given below:

- Plasma Desktop for mouse or keyboard computing devices like desktops or laptops.

- Plasma Mobile for phones.

- Plasma Bigscreen for all the TVs and set-top boxes including voice interaction.

- Plasma Nano for a minimal shell for embedded and touch-enabled devices, like IoT or automotive.

FEATURES OF KDE PLASMA

KDE Plasma is packed with features that users might not know about. We have been using the Plasma Desktop for many years now and still finding new cool features. Here is a list of cool features of KDE Plasma.

Before going forward, you need to frequently know the term "Super Key" in this section since it is often used in these features. The Super key is defined as the key that usually displays the Windows logo for those unfamiliar with this term. It has many other names, such as the Meta Key, Mod4 Key, Windows Key, Logo Key, and others.

KRunner

KRunner is a feature of Plasma. There are a few methods to activate it, but the helpful shortcut using is Alt + Space, and once started, you can do all stuff. You can even launch applications, search for files, run commands, and more.

There are various plugins to expand the functionality of KRunner. You can also disable default plugins if you want to.

ADVANTAGES OF KDE

KDE stood for Kool Desktop Environment but is now known by many as the K Desktop Environment. It is powerfully flexible.

- **Integration:** KDE is well work with many applications of all kinds. There is no need to write an application for KDE, and all of the applications that are part of the GNOME desktop also work fine in KDE. Applications such as the Thunderbird email application and the Firefox web browser work well on the KDE desktop as any on others.

- **Looks:** Sometimes, I want to set colors and looks to suit my moods. Icons, widgets, fonts, pointers, window decorations, and more can also change, and you can download and install new ones. Window decorations mean the look of the borders and buttons on the window frame. At the same time, widgets are the buttons sliders of the applications within the windows.

- **Flexibility:** More importantly than just how it looks, you can change how KDE works. Double clicks to open files and folders with Bluetooth and other connectivity can configure easily, and power management can also be adjusted. KDE allows you to define the functions of the mouse buttons, windows behave, how to deal with new devices.

- **Konsole:** It is a terminal emulator for the desktop. It was written for KDE, but it even can run on other desktops. The most helpful feature is that the Konsole window allows for multiple tabs with a separate terminal session in each tab. You can log in to the localhost as root in the terminal of one tab, a non-root user in another tab, different hosts for two or three other tabs, and switch between them by clicking on the desired tab. You can open with sessions for root on my localhost, a root session on my web and email server, and a local.

- **Multiple desktops:** We have been working on multiple desktops for years with KDE and usually have one main desktop we use for specific user stuff like email, web browsing, and writing documents like this one. We use another desktop to develop new scripts, modify old ones, and test them in virtual machines. It helps us keep things separate and organized to find something reasonably easily.

- **Workflow:** KDE takes a more conservative approach and focuses heavily on aesthetics, sometimes even at the cost of productivity. It is highly customizable, means that you can move panels, add or delete components, and even lets users control the window borders, something you won't find in GNOME.

- **Userbase:** KDE is also picking up pace, thanks to the large-scale user dissatisfaction with GNOME 3. Many users are migrating to other distros, mainly KDE. It's an excellent place for beginners to get into Linux, owning its resemblance to Windows.

CHAPTER SUMMARY

In this chapter, we have covered some KDE distros' basic knowledge and touched on other KDE-based distros like Fedora, openSUSE, Ubuntu, Zorin OS, Majora Edition, etc. You will have learned about KDE versions' history and simple use terms like GUI, CLI, and TUI.

CHAPTER 2

Installation of KDE

IN THIS CHAPTER

➢ Installation of KDE Neon

➢ Live images

➢ Installation of VirtualBox

➢ Introduction KDE Neon

➢ An overview of the KDE desktop environment

In the last chapter, we have covered the basics of KDE distro with its features and advantages. Now we will learn how to install the KDE Neon distros on your system. The latest versions of KDE Neon use KDE Plasma 5 as the default desktop environment. KDE allows using a different desktop environment with a different layout and features like search optimization, improved graphics rendering, and built-in Google Docs support.

INSTALLATION OF KDE NEON

How to Install the KDE Neon Operating System

KDE Neon is a GNU-Linux operating system released, including the latest KDE Plasma desktop version. On another side, if you want to try the newest release of KDE Plasma, try this KDE Neon. This decision of the KDE Project to publish neon is beneficial and easier for those KDE end-users because we do not need to install any upgrade to the currently-installed GNU/Linux system. You can use KDE Neon as LiveCD as a real-installed system or a virtual machine guest. This manual shows step by step to install KDE Neon into your computer.

DOI: 10.1201/9781003309406-2

Download Neon OS

KDE Neon is a method to get the latest KDE Plasma with its related SoftwareSoftware. Their Live Images can be installed from a USB drive to your system hard disk. It is available on a rapidly updated delivery model with installable images and a package archive.

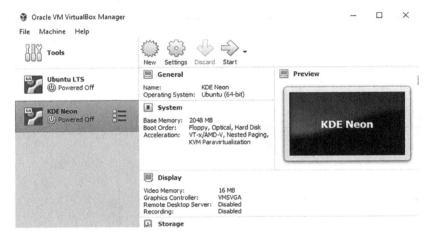

Adding new Virtual Machine

It contains:

- KDE Plasma 5.6

- KDE Frameworks 5.22

- KDE's Visual Design Group selected applications to work well with KDE Plasma: Kate, Firefox, Konsole, KDE Connect, VLC, Spectacle, Dolphin, and Print Manager. It uses the stable version of Ubuntu 16.04LTS.

We build SoftwareSoftware using modern DevOps technologies that scan the latest released sources and quickly integrate that with packaging to make it available to users quickly. It uses technologies that include Jenkins, Ruby, Aptly, Docker, and on-demand cloud computers.

You can obtain a KDE Neon image at the KDE Neon official website https://neon.kde.org/download. It is updated quickly, so you may find the more recent version the day you see it (October 28, 2016). KDE Neon includes the KDE Plasma 5.8, the newest stable LTS version.

On the main download page, such as https://neon.kde.org/download, you see two selections of KDE Neon, User Edition and Developer Edition. Choose the User Edition.

Live Images

Live images are ideal for people who want a clean installation. Use a live image to replace your existing system, install alongside existing operating systems, or simply try KDE neon without affecting their computer.

User Edition ⁶⁴⁻ᵇⁱᵗ

Featuring the latest officially released KDE software on a stable base. Ideal for everyday users.

> User Edition Live/Install Image

PGP signature for verification
Torrent file

Testing Edition ⁶⁴⁻ᵇⁱᵗ

Featuring pre-release KDE software built the same day from bugfix branches. Good for testing. There is no QA. Will contain bugs.

> Testing Edition Live/Install Image

PGP signature for verification
Torrent file

Live images of KDE Neon.

The ISO file name is neon-user-20220113-0956.iso with 1GB size, and the actual download link is https://files.kde.org/neon/images/user/20220113-0956/neon-user-20220113-0956.iso.

LIVE IMAGES

Live images are ideal for those who want a clean installation. You can use a live image to replace your current system, install it alongside existing operating systems, or try KDE Neon without affecting their computer.

Live ISO Image

A Live ISO image is a system on removable media, e.g., a CD/DVD or USB stick. Once built and deployed, it boots off from this media without interfering with other system storage components, making it a helpful pocket system for testing and demo- and debugging purposes.

There are various editions available for KDE Neon.

User Edition (64-bit)

We feature the latest officially released KDE software on a stable base – ideal for everyday users.

Testing Edition (64-bit)
Features pre-release KDE software built the same day from bugfix branches. Good for testing. It will contain bugs.

Unstable Edition (64-bit)
Features pre-release KDE software built the same day from new feature branches. It is suitable for testing. It will contain many bugs.

Developer Edition (64-bit)
Unstable Editon plus development libraries preinstalled.

What Is an Image?

When you read about .iso files, you will often see them as CD images. The term image doesn't refer to a visual image such as a photo or picture but an actual digital copy of the contents of a CD.

You want to use a CD-burning application to burn your .iso file to the CD correctly then inside the application, and there should be a menu option called Burn the Disk Image or something similar. The details can be altered according to the program you use to burn the image. You must select the .iso file, insert a blank CD, and after a few minutes, out will pop a fresh Ubuntu installation CD.

To give you a start, the following.

The following instructions for burning a CD in some popular tools to give you a head start.

In Windows, the following steps are to burn your image Windows:

1. Click right on the icon on the downloaded .iso image and select then open with > Ubuntu Disc Image Burner.

2. Select a writable CD drive from the drop-down box.

3. Click on Burn.

Before You Begin the Installation

Installing a new operating system is a most significant event, and you should make sure that you have thought through what is going to occur. However, Ubuntu and another distro like KDE Neon run well on various hardware. It is valuable to check your hardware components because some bits of hardware do not work well with the Linux distro.

This portion provides some areas for you to investigate and think about; it might save you hours of frustration when something goes wrong, and problems are becoming much less frequent, but they still crop up occasionally.

You can start by researching and documenting your hardware, and the information will prove helpful later on during the installation.

At the absolute, you should know the basics of your system, such as how much RAM you have, what type of mouse and keyboard you have; knowing the storage capacity kind of hard drive you have is crucial because it helps you plan how to divide it for KDE Neon and troubleshoot if problems occur. Whether your mouse uses the USB, a small detail ensures proper pointer configuration something should happen without any problem, but others will be glad you know it if something goes wrong. The other information you have, the better prepared you are for any issues.

Again, the things you want to include the amount of installed memory, the size of the hard drive, the type of mouse, the monitor's capabilities, and the number of installed network interfaces.

Again, the things you want to include the amount of installed memory, the size of the hard drive, the type of mouse, the capabilities of the monitor, and the number of installed network interfaces.

There are many other various ways to install KDE Neon or other Linux:

- You can install it inside a VirtualBox in Windows.

- You can use the Bash on Windows feature to install it inside Windows.

- You can use dual boot neon with Windows so that you can also choose which OS to use at the time the system boots.

- You can replace the Windows system with Ubuntu by wiping it all together from your system.

If you install the default KDE Neon, the system requirements are: Installing KDE Neon requires:

- 64-bit PC (Intel or AMD)

- 2GB memory

- 10GB disk space

There are two methods of installing Ubuntu in your windows laptops:

1. By downloading the .iso file and creating the virtual machine.

2. By burning CD or DVD with .iso file.

Let's discuss both methods one by one, so first by creating the virtual machine of Ubuntu in VirtualBox.

- First, download the VirtualBox from its official website, https://www
.virtualbox.org/wiki/Downloads. It could take some time to download but install it on your Windows operating system once it gets downloaded.

Name of the website.

- Next, you have to click the download button to get the VirtualBox.

VirtualBox is being actively developed with frequent releases and has an ever growing list of features, supported guest operating systems and platforms it runs on. VirtualBox is a community effort backed by a dedicated company: everyone is encouraged to contribute while Oracle ensures the product always meets professional quality criteria.

Name of the website.

- Once you click on this button, .exe of virtualBox file. A new window will open as shown below.

VirtualBox binaries

By downloading, you agree to the terms and conditions of the respective license.

If you're looking for the latest VirtualBox 6.0 packages, see VirtualBox 6.0 builds. Please also use version 6.0 if you need to run VMs with software virtualization, as this has been discontinued in 6.1. Version 6.0 will remain supported until July 2020.

If you're looking for the latest VirtualBox 5.2 packages, see VirtualBox 5.2 builds. Please also use version 5.2 if you still need support for 32-bit hosts, as this has been discontinued in 6.0. Version 5.2 will remain supported until July 2020.

VirtualBox 6.1.30 platform packages

- ⇨Windows hosts
- ⇨OS X hosts
- Linux distributions
- ⇨Solaris hosts
- ⇨Solaris 11 IPS hosts

The binaries are released under the terms of the GPL version 2.

See the changelog for what has changed.

You might want to compare the checksums to verify the integrity of downloaded packages. The SHA256 checksums should be favored as the MD5 algorithm must be treated as insecure!

- SHA256 checksums, MD5 checksums

Activate Windows

New of the website.

You can see the following links. It is just a .exe file based on the various operating systems such as:

- VirtualBox 6.1.30 platform packages
- Windows hosts
- OS X hosts
- Linux distributions
- Solaris hosts
- Solaris 11 IPS hosts

When you click on the links, you will get a .exe file as per your system, whether Windows, Linux, macOS, etc.

- After that, you need to install it by running the .exe file you have already installed. For steps on how to download and install VirtualBox, follow the link. Windows 10 is available on Microsoft's official web page. Here you will either have to log in or register for Windows inside a program to gain access to the download. Make sure you download the ISO.

  After clicking on the icon, the window will open.

VirtualBox Installation Step 1.

- Click on Next on the button and make everything as is it.

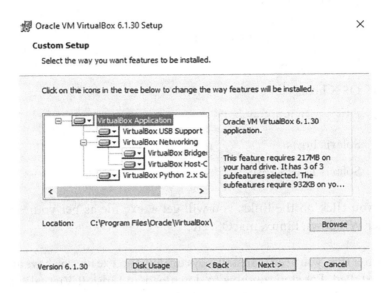

VirtualBox Installation Step 2.

- The next window will be shown as,

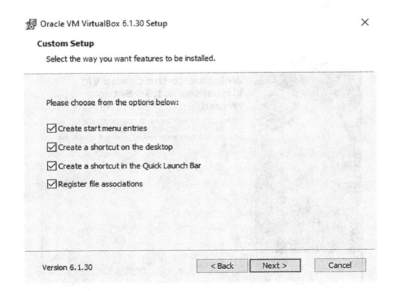

VirtualBox Installation Step 3.

- Again you will get popup windows as a custom setup; click on Yes.

VirtualBox Installation Step 4.

- Then you will get new popup windows with a progress bar. It might take a while to start the bar.

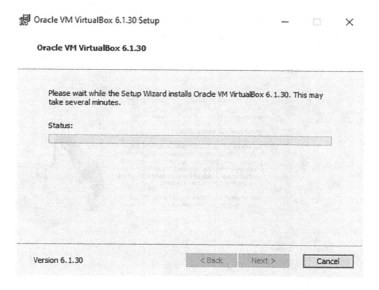

VirtualBox Installation Step 5.

- Windows. After this, your virtualBox installation is completed.

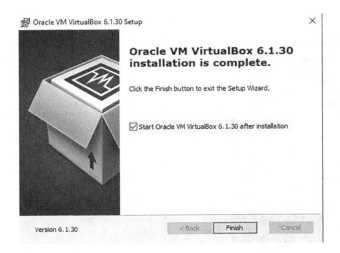

VirtualBox Installation Step 6.

VIRTUALBOX

All the above steps are related to the VirtualBox downloading and installation. So now we are going to create the new virtual machine in the virtualBox. Here the steps are given below:

- Open VirtualBox and select "new machine." You can be able to do this once you've installed VirtualBox Screen.

VirtualBox Manager Screen.

- Click on the New button, and then you will see Name and operating System the Type in "KDE Neon" into the text box. You can type in or choose a different name for the Operating System if you prefer. Once this is done, select "Linux" on the first scroll menu, and then select "Ubuntu LTS" from the version box (second scroll box).

VirtualBox KDE Neon installation and adding name of KDE Neon.

- Select how much RAM you would like to give the KDE Neon machine. When the windows wizards ask you how much RAM to provide the machine, then you have to provide the default amount of RAM should be fine, but if you have a lesser or limited RAM, then adjusting using the slider is good for you.

Selecting RAM for KDE Neon installation.

- Do not select anything when the wizard window asks about a new virtual hard disk. By default, "Create a Virtual hard disk" would be chosen. Just simply select "Next."

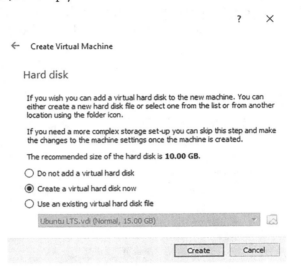

Add virtual hard disk.

- Select the disk file type as VDI (VirtualBox Disk Image), then click Next.

Select hard disk file type.

- Set your disk space for the hard drive. The wizard asks you to set the disk space for your physical hard drive.

Storage on physical hard disk.

- You can select a dynamically allocated or a fixed size also may choose either; it is often better to choose a limited size, as it is usually faster and more stable.

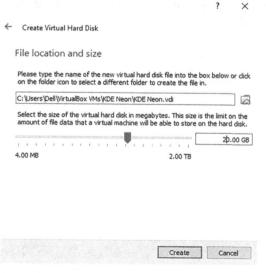

File location and size.

- Select disk size 20 gigabytes. It should be selected as a minimum, but the more space, the merrier. Then click on the setting of the virtual-Box. The dialog will open then you can see the number of options on the left of the window, such as available system, display, etc. Just click on the system and change the following setting, like remove the tick in the front of the floppy and click OK.

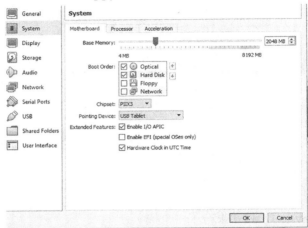

Setting of floppy disk.

- Now move to another option, that is storage. Click on the first button and add the .iso file of the Ubuntu that you already download from their official website in it. After adding it, click on the Choose button and then OK.

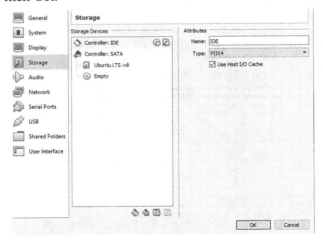

Storage setting in a virtual setting.

Then the file will be added to your virtual machine.

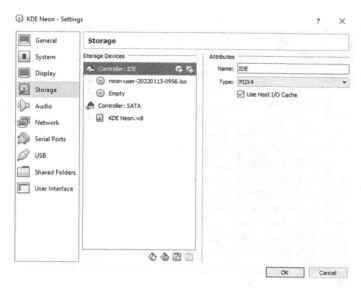

Adding KDE neon .iso file.

- Run the KDE Neon Virtual Machine by double-clicking. The window will be like

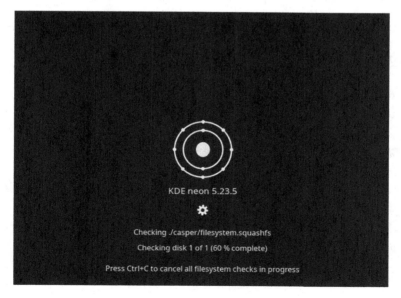

Loading KDE neon .iso file.

- When the desktop gets loaded, press the Install System button.

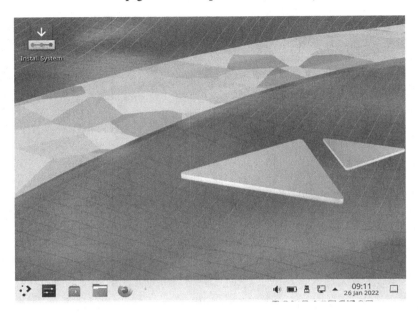

Installation icon appears on the screen.

- You will see the Welcome to the KDE Neon installer in the following window. Select your preferred language and click Next.

Select your preferred language.

- Select the location, i.e., region, location, and zone, and then click Next.

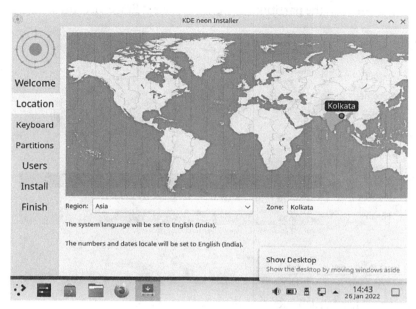

Select the appropriate location.

Select the desired Keyboard Layout at the next screen and click Next.

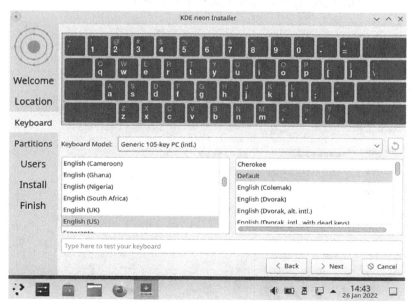

Select the desired keyboard layout.

- As you have created a new virtual hard disk for your KDE Neon virtual machine, on the partitions screen, then select Erase disk and click Next.

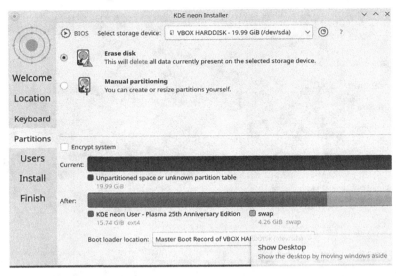

New virtual hard disk for KDE Neon virtual machine.

- Enter the required credentials in all the fields to create a new user for the KDE Neon system, and then click Install.

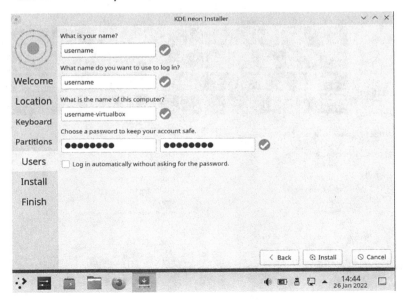

Enter the details.

- The installation will now begin. It might take some time.

Installation of KDE Neon.

- When the installation gets completed, press the Done button, KDE Neon will restart.

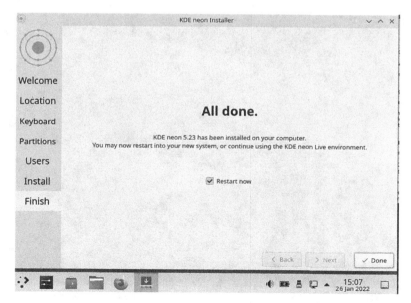

Installation is completed.

- Now reboot your system, you will see the following login screen.

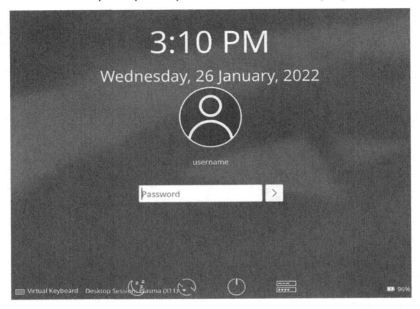

Login screen of KDE Neon.

- Enter your system password and log into your KDE Neon system.

First screen of KDE Neon.

INTRODUCTION TO KDE NEON

KDE Neon is a GNU-Linux system made by the free software project KDE, which shows the latest KDE Plasma desktop technology. It is fundamentally the latest Ubuntu LTS release with updated Qt and KDE repositories on top. The OS is available in four different variants: The "User" edition, the "Testing" edition, the "Unstable" edition, and the "Developer" edition, which is the "Unstable" release edition with development libraries preinstalled. It can be used directly from a live USB or installed using a friendly installer.

KDE Neon's live image boots into a functional KDE Plasma desktop with an "Install neon" icon in the upper left corner. Starting the installation, the installer is straightforward. It asks you to choose language, keyboard if you have it, then asks about SoftwareSoftware. An option is called "Install third-party software for graphics and Wi-Fi hardware and additional media formats." Enabling this option installs proprietary drivers and free software packages for multimedia, which are covered by patents in some parts of the world.

AN OVERVIEW OF THE KDE DESKTOP ENVIRONMENT

KDE serves several essential roles in the Linux community:

- It is one of the best free software projects around and proves its benefits.

- It is the default desktop environment for several Linux distributions, giving them a powerful, modern UI.

- It supplies the community with many free applications, from games to audio players to any office programs. Even if you do not use KDE before as your desktop environment, you're still free to take advantage of its apps.

- It provides developers who aren't formal project members with a great head start for developing their applications in KDE.

This is a guide to the KDE Plasma desktop environment within Linux. Plasma is more than just a desktop-like other full-featured Linux desktop environment. It's a complete application ecosystem with everything you'd need on a typical day using your computer. The KDE ecosystem is easily among the most active in the open source world.

This guide will cover the Plasma desktop, including activities, widgets, and customization. It will dive into typical KDE applications that usually come with Plasma, including multimedia apps, internet connection sharing, graphics image editing. It should serve as a complete primer to get you up and running with KDE Plasma on Linux PC.

This overview guide won't go into depth about any of the tools, but it provides essential information highlighting the basic features.

The Desktop

The image on the page shows the default KDE Plasma desktop. The wallpaper is bright and vibrant. There will be a single panel at the bottom and on the top left is a small icon with three lines on it. The panel has the various icons in the bottom left corner as given below:

- The application launcher will be like,

Application launcher.

- Virtual Workspace selector

    The bottom right corner has some icons and indicators such as,

    - Notifications

    - Updates

    - Volume

    - Battery

    - Networks

- Panel Editor (^ icon)
- Clock

The menu has the following tabs:

- Applications
- Places
- Sleep
- Restart
- Shut Down
- Switch user
- Logout
- Lock

The favorites tab has a list of favorite programs. You can select an icon that brings up the application. There is a search bar at the top of the tabs to search by name. You can also remove an item from the favorites list by right-clicking on the menu. You can sort your favorites menu alphabetically from a to z or z to a.

The applications tab starts with a list as follows:

- Favorites
- Application
- Graphics
- Internet
- Multimedia
- Office
- Settings
- System
- Utilities
- Help center

The list of categories is customizable.

Choosing a category displays the applications within the category. You can run any application by clicking on the icon. You can even pin the application to the favorites list by right-clicking or by selecting add to favorites.

The tab has a section called applications, having system settings and run commands. The other section on the tab is called places. It lists the home folder, network folder, root folder, waste bin, and recently opened folders. If you enter a removable drive, it gets appear in a section at the bottom of the removable tab.

The history tab gives a list of recently used applications and documents. You can also clear the history by right-clicking on the menu or by selecting clear history.

The left tab has session and system settings. The session settings let the user log out, lock the computer or switch users, whereas the system settings let you turn off the computer, reboot it, or make it sleep.

Widgets

Widgets can add to the desktop or panel. Some widgets are added to the panel, and some are better suited to the desktop.

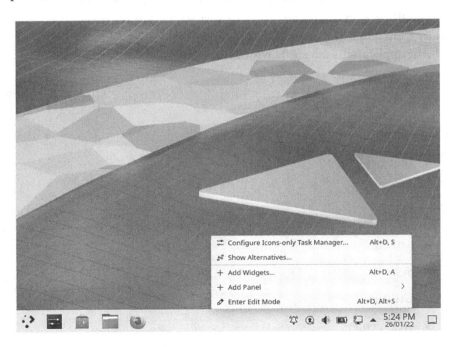

Adding widgets.

KDE Plasma Widgets

To add widgets to the panel, you need to click on the panel settings icon in the bottom right and choose your widget. To add widgets to the main desktop, just right-click and select add widget. You can add widgets by clicking the icon in the top left corner and selecting add widget.

Regardless of which widget option you choose, the result is the same. A list of widgets will appear on the left of the screen, which you can drag into position either on the desktop or on the panel.

The image shows a couple of the widgets such as a clock, dashboard icon, and a folder view. Here are a few more widgets that are available:

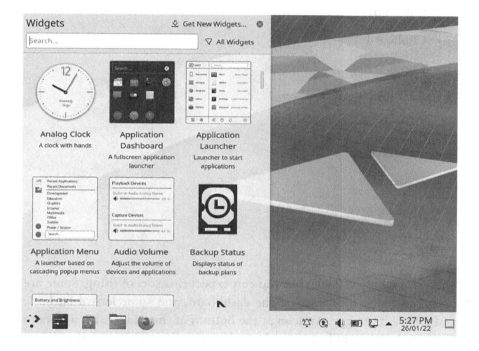

Various widgets.

Here is the list of the following widgets available in KDE Neon:

- **Activities icon:** It used to show the activities menu

- **Activities bar:** It used for switching activities

- Analog clock

- **Dashboard:** Bit like the Ubuntu Dash

- **Application launcher:** The menu

- **Application menu:** Alternative menu

- Audio volume

- Battery

- Bluetooth

- Calculator

- Calendar

- Clipboard

- Comic strip

- CPU load monitor

- Device notifier

- Digital clock

- Folder view

- Media player

- Notes

There are more available, but you can expect this sort of thing. Some are useful and look nice, such as the dashboard, and some look a bit basic and a little bit buggy. An icon at the bottom of the widgets list allows to download and install more widgets. You can download Gmail notifiers and Yahoo weather widgets.

Activities

KDE has a concept called activities. They are a new way of handling workspaces because each activity can have multiple workspaces. Activities let you break your desktops down into features. For example, if you do a lot of graphics work, you might choose to have an activity called graphics. You can have multiple workspaces within the graphics activity, but each one is geared toward graphics. A more helpful activity would be for presentations. When showing a presentation, you want the screen to remain on without going to sleep or the screensaver.

You could have a presentation activity with the settings set to never timeout. Your default activity can be a standard desktop that times out and shows the screensaver after a short period of use.

Configuring KDE

The KDE desktop is highly customizable. It can add different widgets and create activities you can change every other part of the desktop experience. You can also modify the desktop wallpaper by right-clicking and choosing desktop settings.

It lets you choose the desktop wallpaper and not much more. Select the menu and select system settings to get into the simple configuration settings. You will see the options for the following categories:

- Appearance

- Workspace

- Personalization

- Network

- Hardware

- System Administration

The appearance settings let you change the theme and splash screen. You can also customize cursors, icons, fonts, and application styles.

The workspace settings have many settings, including turning on and off dozens of desktop effects such as mouse animation functions, fade desktop, magnifiers, zoom, etc.

You can also add hotspots for each workspace so that when you click into a particular corner, an action happens, such as an application loads. Personalization lets you customize things about user managers, notifications, and default applications. Networks let you configure proxy servers, SSL certificates, Bluetooth, and Windows shares.

The "K" Menu

The "K" menu at the left of the panel is like the "Start" menu. It allows you to browse all your installed GUI applications. KDE contains some categories to allow organizing things a bit easier, such as,

- Education

- Games

- Internet

- Multimedia

- Office

- Settings

- System

- Lost and Found

Task Manager

It is a list of presently running applications. It can show the icon the title of each application currently opened.

- The "active" application is highlighted with a border.

- Clicking on an application other than the current one will make the selected one "active."

- Right-clicking on an application gives of maximizing, minimizing, or closing.

System Tray

The System Tray is also similar to what you'd find in Windows or Mac OS. Programs that run in the background only require quick input or more system-related ones.

Adding Widgets to Panels

You can add some widgets to panels as well as the desktop. To add one, right-click on the panel instead of the desktop background. You may get some options for an already-present widget, but there will be a menu item titled "Panel Options," within which you'll find the "Add Widgets" item.

Various panel.

System Settings

KDE has "System Settings," which has a similar UI to the "System Preferences" of Mac OS X. Each of the "configuration modules" is arranged into groupings.

Shortcuts and Gestures

Go to the "Shortcuts and Gestures" in the "Common Appearance and Behavior" group. KDE uses keyboard shortcuts that include the following modules:

- **Standard Keyboard Shortcuts:** It lets set or modify the shortcuts for commands common across many applications. Most applications use the "Control" key by default.

- **Global Keyboard Shortcuts:** These shortcuts work regardless of which application you are currently in.

- **Custom Shortcuts:** You can set up shortcuts for about any program, including setting up gestures for them.

CHAPTER SUMMARY

This chapter presents an overview guide to the KDE Plasma desktop environment within Linux. Plasma is more than just a desktop - like other full-featured Linux desktop environments. It's a complete application ecosystem with everything you'd need on a typical day using your computer. The KDE ecosystem is easily among the most active in the open source world.

This guide has covered the Plasma desktop, including activities, widgets, and customization. It will also dive into typical KDE applications that usually come with Plasma. That includes multimedia apps, internet connection and sharing, and graphics and image editing.

CHAPTER 3

Applications

➢ KDE Advanced Text Editor application

➢ Kdenlive application

➢ Document viewer – Okular application

➢ K3b application

➢ KMail application

➢ Korganizer application

➢ And more

In Chapter 2, we have covered how to install the KDE Neon distro on a system. We use .iso file to install the KDE Neon in VirtualBox Machine.

This chapter discusses the KDE Neon application and how it works, installed in your system, user interface guide, feature, and more. Again we will tell you what is KDE Neon as follows.

Application software, known as an "app," is computer software designed to help users perform specific tasks. Examples: enterprise software, other accounting software, office suites like Libre, graphics, and media player software. Many application programs deal with documents. Apps can be bundled with the program and its software or published separately.

Application software comes with system software and middleware, which manage and integrate the system's capabilities, but don't directly

DOI: 10.1201/9781003309406-3

apply the performance of tasks that benefit the user. The software serves the application, which in turn helps the user.

Similar relationships apply in other fields. For example, rail tracks similarly support trains, allowing the trains to transport passengers. In-mall does not provide the merchandise a shopper seeks but provides space and services for retailers that serve the shopper.

Application software has the power of a particular computing system software to a specific purpose. Some applications, such as Microsoft Office, are available in versions for different platforms, but others have narrower requirements. For example, a Geography application for Windows, an Android application for education, or Linux gaming. Sometimes a new and popular application runs on one platform, increasing the desirability of that platform. It is called a killer application.

APPLICATION SOFTWARE CLASSIFICATION

The application falls into the following two general categories:

- Horizontal applications
- Vertical applications

Horizontal applications are widespread in departments or companies. Vertical applications are products designed for a particular type of business or division in a company.

What Is KDE Neon?

KDE Neon is a Linux distribution designed by KDE based on the most Ubuntu (LTS) release, bundled with a set of additional software containing the latest 64-bit versions of the KDE Plasma 5 desktop environment, Qt 5 toolkit, and other consistent KDE software. It was first announced in June 2016 by Kubuntu founder Jonathan Riddell from Canonical Ltd.

It is offered in stable and development variants; the User Edition is a stable release featuring the latest KDE packages that have passed quality warranty. The Testing, Unstable, and Developer Edition branches use KDE packages' newest beta and unstable nightly releases.

There are various applications to choose from in distribution repositories. Nevertheless, only KDE Neon apps will have buttons in the window border and sufficiently use the application menu button at the top of the screen. Since some software are not labeled, new and seasoned Linux users alike can have a difficult time finding additional KDE Neon apps. Here's a list of several programs that were not preinstalled with your distribution.

We can install application in any Linux distro using apt and snap. Let's discuss both terms before installation.

Compared to other operating systems, Linux takes various approaches to software management. The software in Linux is organized in repositories. Repositories can contain applications and all the dependencies necessary to run.

While using repositories is convenient for reasons, it presents an obstacle for users who are not tech-savvy. Several alternative packaging systems have been created to make the Linux experience more user-friendly over the past couple of years.

What Is Snap?

Snap is a software package that uses self-contained packages known as snaps to deliver software to users. Snaps have all the dependencies a program requires in a single package. The app is agnostic that can natively run on any Linux distribution that supports Snap.

While APT mainly obtains packages from a distribution's official repositories, Snap enables other developers to deliver their apps to users via the Snap Store. Developers can also publish snaps instantly on their websites.

The tool used in snap management is called snapd. It enables a system to run snap packages. Users can interact with snapd by using the snap client.

What Is APT?

APT stands for Advanced Package Tool. It is a software package manager for installing and removing packages on Debian-based systems. APT can automate upgrading, installing, retrieving, configuring, and removing packages. It is a front-end of Debian base package management system dpkg.

The main benefit of APT is the way it handles software dependencies. After a user runs a command to install a package, it can search the repositories for the package's dependencies and establish those not already installed on the system.

The tool that APT mainly uses to interface with users is apt. The utility offers the most popular apt-get and apt-cache commands, considered less user-friendly.

The following table explains the terminology of both apt and snap:

Terminology	Snap	APT
Type of package	.snap	.deb
Name of the tool	snapd	APT
CLI tool	snap	Apt
Available in	Snap Store	Debian repositories
Installation Size	Larger	Smaller
Multiple installations	Possible	Not possible
Multiple version installations	Possible	Not possible

Here is a list of applications designed for use with the KDE Neon desktop environment.

KDE ADVANCED TEXT EDITOR APPLICATION

Installing Kate as a Snap Package

A snap package is a universal Linux package that you can enjoy irrespective of the distro. It is a self-contained software package that includes all dependencies needed to run the application.

If the snapd package is not installed, you can install it by running the following command:

```
$ sudo apt install snapd
username@username-virtualbox:~$ sudo apt install snapd
```

```
[sudo] password for username:
Reading package lists Done
Building dependency tree    Done
Reading state information Done
snapd is already the new version (2.51.1+20.04ubuntu2).
snapd set to manually installed.
Starting pkgProblemResolver with broken count: 0
Starting 2 pkgProblemResolver with broken count: 0
Done
The following packages were installed and are no longer
required:
    gstreamer1.0-nice gstreamer1.0-plugins-bad gstreamer1.0-
    plugins-good gstreamer1.0-x libbs2b0
```

The Snap version of the Kate Editor application can be used on any Linux distribution that has Snap support.

Enable Snaps and Install a Kate Text Editor

Snaps applications are packaged with dependencies to run on all popular Linux distributions from a single build. They update automatically and roll back gracefully.

Snaps are can installable from the Snap Store, an app store with an audience of millions.

Enable snapd in Terminal

Snap can install from the command line. Open the Konsole terminal window and enter the following:

```
$ sudo apt update
$ sudo apt install snapd
```

To install kate, use the following command:

```
$ sudo snap install kate –classic
username@username-virtualbox:~$ sudo snap install kate
--classic
[sudo] password for username:
2022-01-26T17:55:02+05:30 INFO Waiting for automatic snapd
restart...
kate 21.08.0 from KDE* installed
```

It is a multi-document, multi-view text editor by KDE. It features code folding, syntax highlighting, dynamic word wrap, an embedded console, an extensive plugin interface, and preliminary scripting support.

Installing Kate from Ubuntu Repositories

Installing Kate Editor from repositories is relatively straightforward and takes only a few minutes to complete.

Open a terminal using a keyboard shortcut, i.e., CTRL+ALT+T, and execute the below to update packages.

```
$ sudo apt update && sudo apt upgrade
```

```
username@username-virtualbox:~$ sudo apt install snapd
[sudo] password for username:
Reading package lists Done
Building dependency tree Done
```

```
Reading state information Done
snapd is already the new version (2.51.1+20.04ubuntu2).
snapd set to manually installed.
Starting pkgProblemResolver with broken count: 0
Starting 2 pkgProblemResolver with broken count: 0
Done
The following packages were installed and are no longer
required:
  gstreamer1.0-nice gstreamer1.0-plugins-bad gstreamer1.0-
plugins-good gstreamer1.0-x libbs2b0
```

Now execute the given command to install the Kate package.

```
$ sudo apt install kate
```

```
username@username-virtualbox:~$ sudo apt  install kate
Reading package lists... Done
Building dependency tree
Reading state information... Done
Starting pkgProblemResolver with broken count: 0
Starting 2 pkgProblemResolver with broken count: 0
Done
The following packages were installed and are no longer
required:
  gstreamer1.0-nice gstreamer1.0-plugins-bad gstreamer1.0-
plugins-good gstreamer1.0-x libbs2b0
  libde265-0 libdv4 libfarstream-0.2-5 libfftw3-double3
libflite1 libfluidsynth2 libgadu3
  libgssdp-1.2-0 libgstreamer-plugins-bad1.0-0
libgstreamer-plugins-good1.0-0 libgupnp-1.2-0
  libgupnp-igd-1.0-4 libiec61883-0 libinstpatch-1.0-2
liblilv-0-0 libmeanwhile1
```

Features:

- MDI, window splitting, window tabbing

- Spell checking

- CR, CRLF, LF newline support

- Encoding support (utf-8, utf-16, ASCII, etc.)

- Encoding conversion

- Regular expression-based find and replace

- Powerful syntax highlighting and bracket matching
- Code and text folding
- Infinite undo/redo support
- Block selection mode
- Auto indentation
- Auto-completion support
- Shell integration
- Support comprehensive protocol, such as HTTP, FTP, ssh, WebDAV, etc., using kioslaves
- Support plugin architecture for the application and editor component
- Scriptable using JavaScript
- Integrated command line
- Customizable shortcuts

The license used in Kate is GPL-2.0+.

The first screen of Kate text editor is given below.

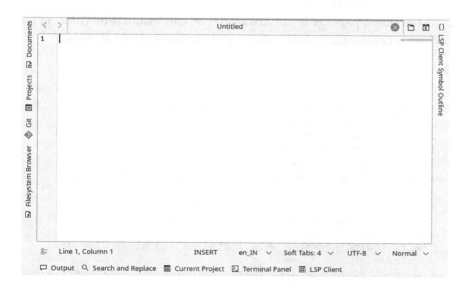

Kate Text Editor window.

How to Uninstall Kate Text Editor

If you want to uninstall the Kate application via Snap, use and type the following command:

```
$ sudo snap remove kate
```

Run the following command if you have installed Kate via apt:

```
$ sudo apt remove kate
```

KDENLIVE APPLICATION

Kdenlive is an open source video editor. The project was started in 2003. It is built on Qt and the KDE Frameworks libraries. Most video processing is done by the MLT Framework, which relies on many other open source projects like FFmpeg, frei0r, movit, ladspa, sox, etc. A small team develops Kdenlive, and new contributors are welcome.

Kdenlive is a nonlinear editor for video which is based on the MLT framework. It can accept various audio and video formats, allowing you to add effects, transitions, and render into the layout of your choice.

Installing Kdenlive as a Snap Package

A snap package is a universal Linux package that you can enjoy irrespective of the distro. It is a self-contained software package that includes all dependencies needed to run the application.

If the snapd package is not installed, you can install it by running the following command:

```
$ sudo apt install snapd
```

```
username@username-virtualbox:~$ sudo apt install snapd
[sudo] password for username:
Reading package lists Done
Building dependency tree        Done
Reading state information Done
snapd is already the new version (2.51.1+20.04ubuntu2).
snapd set to manually installed.
Starting pkgProblemResolver with broken count: 0
Starting 2 pkgProblemResolver with broken count: 0
Done
The following packages were installed and are no longer
required:
  gstreamer1.0-nice gstreamer1.0-plugins-bad gstreamer1.0-
plugins-good gstreamer1.0-x libbs2b0
```

The Snap version of the kdenlive application can be used on any Linux distribution that has Snap support.

Enable Snaps and Install a Kdenlive Text Editor

Snaps applications are packaged with dependencies to run on all popular Linux distributions from a single build. They update automatically and roll back gracefully.

Snaps are can installable from the Snap Store, an app store with an audience of millions.

Enable snapd in Terminal

Snap can install from the command line. Open the Konsole terminal window and enter the following:

```
$ sudo apt update
$ sudo apt install snapd
```

To install kdenlive, use the following command:

```
$ sudo snap install kdenlive
```

```
username@username-virtualbox:~$ sudo snap install kdenlive
kdenlive 21.08.3 from KDE* installed
```

It is a multi-document, multi-view text editor by KDE. It features code folding, syntax highlighting, dynamic word wrap, an embedded console, an extensive plugin interface, and preliminary scripting support.

Installing Kdenlive from Ubuntu Repositories

Installing kdenlive from repositories is relatively straightforward and takes only a few minutes to complete.

Open a terminal using a keyboard shortcut, i.e., CTRL+ALT+T, and execute the below to update packages.

```
$ sudo apt update && sudo apt upgrade
```

```
username@username-virtualbox:~$ sudo apt install snapd
[sudo] password for username:
Reading package lists Done
Building dependency tree
```

```
Reading state informatio Done
snapd is already the new version (2.51.1+20.04ubuntu2).
snapd set to manually installed.
Starting pkgProblemResolver with broken count: 0
Starting 2 pkgProblemResolver with broken count: 0
Done
The following packages were installed and are no longer
required:
  gstreamer1.0-nice gstreamer1.0-plugins-bad gstreamer1.0-
plugins-good gstreamer1.0-x libbs2b0
```

Now execute the following command to install the kdenlive package:

```
$ sudo apt install kdenlive
```

```
username@username-virtualbox:~$ sudo apt  install  kdenlive
[sudo] password for username:
Reading package lists... Done
Building dependency tree
Reading state information... Done
kdenlive is already the newest version (4:21.12.1-0xneon+20
.04+focal+release+build45).
Starting pkgProblemResolver with broken count: 0
Starting 2 pkgProblemResolver with broken count: 0
Done
The following packages were installed and are no longer
required:
  gstreamer1.0-nice gstreamer1.0-plugins-bad gstreamer1.0-
plugins-good gstreamer1.0-x
  libde265-0 libfarstream-0.2-5 libfluidsynth2 libgadu3
libgssdp-1.2-0
  libgstreamer-plugins-bad1.0-0 libgstreamer-plugins-
good1.0-0 libgupnp-1.2-0
  libgupnp-igd-1.0-4 libinstpatch-1.0-2 libmeanwhile1
libmjpegutils-2.1-0 libmms0 libmodplug1
  libmpeg2encpp-2.1-0 libmplex2-2.1-0 libnice10 libofa0
libprotobuf-c1 libpurple-bin
  libpurple0 libsoundtouch1 libspandsp2 libsrtp2-1
libusrsctp1 libv4l-0 libv4lconvert0
  libvo-aacenc0 libvo-amrwbenc0 libwildmidi2 libzbar0
libzephyr4 pidgin-data
  timgm6mb-soundfont
Use 'sudo apt autoremove' to remove them.
0 upgraded, 0 latest installed, 0 to remove and 53 not
upgraded.
```

Features:

- Intuitive multitrack interface

- Many effects and transitions

- Color scopes

- Details for kdenlive

- Multitrack video editing

- Configurable interface and shortcuts

- Use any audio/video format

- Keyframeable effects

- Themable interface

- Timeline preview

- Online resources

- Automatic backup

There are various tillers supports.
Create 2D titles for your projects, including:

- Align and Distribute

- Letter-spacing and Line-spacing adjustment

- Rotate and Zoom

- Add images

- It supports template

- Embedded Crawl and Roll tool for text animation

- Unicode decoder

- System font selector including font-family support

- Design features: Color, Shadows, Outlines, and Gradients

Audio and video scopes:

- It can monitor audio levels or check the color scopes to ensure you correctly balance your footage.

- Audio Meter

- Histogram

- Waveform

- Vectorscope

- RGB Parade

The license used in Kate is GPL-2.0+.

The first screen of Kdenlive is given below.

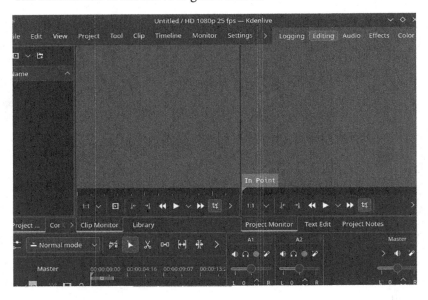

Kdenlive window.

DOCUMENT VIEWER – OKULAR APPLICATION

Okular is a document viewer developed by the KDE community and based on Qt and KDE Frameworks libraries and distributed as part of the KDE Applications bundle. Its origin is from KPDF, and it replaces KPDF, KFax, KFaxview, KGhostView, and KDVI in KDE 4. Its functionality can be merged in other applications. It works on multiple platforms but is not limited to Linux, Windows, Mac OS X, *BSD, etc.

Installing Okular as a Snap Package

A snap package is a universal Linux package that you can enjoy irrespective of the distro. It is a self-contained software package that includes all dependencies needed to run the application.

If the snapd package is not installed, you can install it by running the following command:

```
$ sudo apt install snapd
```

```
username@username-virtualbox:~$ sudo apt install snapd
[sudo] password for username:
Reading package lists... Done
Building dependency tree  Done
Reading state information... Done
snapd is already the new version (2.51.1+20.04ubuntu2).
snapd set to manually installed.
Starting pkgProblemResolver with broken count: 0
Starting 2 pkgProblemResolver with broken count: 0
Done
The following packages were installed and are no longer
required:
  gstreamer1.0-nice gstreamer1.0-plugins-bad gstreamer1.0-
plugins-good gstreamer1.0-x libbs2b0
```

The Snap version of the Okular application can be used on any Linux distribution that has Snap support.

Enable Snaps and Install Okular

Snaps applications are packaged with dependencies to run on all popular Linux distributions from a single build. They update automatically and roll back gracefully.

Snaps are can installable from the Snap Store, an app store with an audience of millions.

Enable snapd in Terminal

Snap can install from the command line. Open the Konsole terminal window and enter the following command:

```
$ sudo apt update
$ sudo apt install snapd
```

To install Okular, use the following command:

```
$ sudo snap install Okular
```

```
username@username-virtualbox:~$ sudo snap install Okular
Okular 21.08.3 from KDE* installed
```

It is a multi-document, multi-view text editor by KDE. It features code folding, syntax highlighting, dynamic word wrap, an embedded console, an extensive plugin interface, and preliminary scripting support.

Installing Okular from Ubuntu Repositories

Installing Okular from repositories is relatively straightforward and takes only a few minutes to complete.

Open a terminal using a keyboard shortcut, i.e., CTRL+ALT+T, and execute the below to update packages.

```
$ sudo apt update && sudo apt upgrade
```

```
username@username-virtualbox:~$ sudo apt install snapd
[sudo] password for username:
Reading package lists... Done
Building dependency tree        Done
Reading state information... Done
snapd is already the new version (2.51.1+20.04ubuntu2).
snapd set to manually installed.
Starting pkgProblemResolver with broken count: 0
Starting 2 pkgProblemResolver with broken count: 0
Done
The following packages were installed and are no longer
required:
  gstreamer1.0-nice gstreamer1.0-plugins-bad gstreamer1.0-
plugins-good gstreamer1.0-x libbs2b0
```

Now execute the given command to install the Okular package.

```
$ sudo apt install Okular
```

```
username@username-virtualbox:~$ sudo apt  install  Okular
[sudo] password for username:
Reading package lists... Done
```

```
Building dependency tree
Reading state information... Done
Okular is already the newest version (4:21.12.1-0xneon+20.0
4+focal+release+build45).
Starting pkgProblemResolver with broken count: 0
Starting 2 pkgProblemResolver with broken count: 0
Done
The following packages were installed and are no longer
required:
  gstreamer1.0-nice gstreamer1.0-plugins-bad gstreamer1.0-
plugins-good gstreamer1.0-x
  libde265-0 libfarstream-0.2-5 libfluidsynth2 libgadu3
libgssdp-1.2-0
  libgstreamer-plugins-bad1.0-0 libgstreamer-plugins-
good1.0-0 libgupnp-1.2-0
  libgupnp-igd-1.0-4 libinstpatch-1.0-2 libmeanwhile1
libmjpegutils-2.1-0 libmms0 libmodplug1
  libmpeg2encpp-2.1-0 libmplex2-2.1-0 libnice10 libofa0
libprotobuf-c1 libpurple-bin
  libpurple0 libsoundtouch1 libspandsp2 libsrtp2-1
libusrsctp1 libv4l-0 libv4lconvert0
  libvo-aacenc0 libvo-amrwbenc0 libwildmidi2 libzbar0
libzephyr4 pidgin-data
  timgm6mb-soundfont
Use 'sudo apt autoremove' to remove them.
0 upgraded, 0 new installed, 0 to remove and 53 not upgraded.
```

Features:

- Sidebar with contents, thumbnails, reviews, and bookmarks

- Annotations support

- File format support

It supports the following file formats:

- Portable Document Format (PDF) with the Poppler backend

- PostScript with the libspectre backend

- Tagged Image File Format (TIFF) with the libTIFF backend

- Microsoft Compiled HTML Help (CHM) with the libCHM backend

- DjVu with the DjVuLibre backend

- Device-independent file format (DVI)

- XML Paper Specification (XPS)

- OpenDocument format (ODF) (only OpenDocument Text)

- FictionBook (*.fb2)

- ComicBook

- Plucker

- ePub

- Mobipocket

- Various image formats, such as JPG

- Markdown

The first screen of Okular is given below,

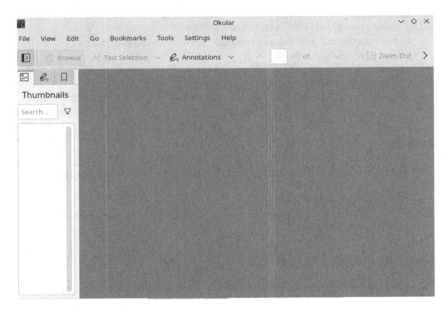

Okular window.

DOLPHIN APPLICATION

It is a file manager that allows one to navigate and browse the contents of hard drives, USB sticks, SD cards, and creating, moving, or deleting files and folders is fast and straightforward.

It contains many productivity features that save you time. The multiple tabs and split-view features allow navigating multiple folders simultaneously, and you can easily drag and drop files between views to move or copy them. Dolphin's right-click menu provides many quick actions that let you compress, share, and duplicate files, among many other things. You can also add your custom actions.

It is lightweight, and you can adapt it to specific needs means that you can carry out your file management precisely the way you want to. It supports three different view modes:

- A tree view

- A more detailed view

- A classic grid view

You can configure Dolphin's behavior.

It can display files and folders from many Internet cloud services and rest remote machines as if they were right there on desktop.

Dolphin also has an integrated terminal that allows you to run commands on the current folder. You can extend the capabilities even further with powerful plugins to adapt them to the workflow. You can use the git plugin to interact with git repositories, the Nextcloud plugin to synchronize your files online, and much more.

Installing Dolphin as a Snap Package

A snap package is a universal Linux package that you can enjoy irrespective of the distro. It is a self-contained software package that includes all dependencies needed to run the application.

If the snapd package is not installed, you can install it by running the following command:

```
$ sudo apt install snapd
```

```
username@username-virtualbox:~$ sudo apt install snapd
[sudo] password for username:
Reading package lists... Done
Building dependency tree      Done
Reading state information... Done
snapd is already the new version (2.51.1+20.04ubuntu2).
```

```
snapd set to manually installed.
Starting pkgProblemResolver with broken count: 0
Starting 2 pkgProblemResolver with broken count: 0
Done
The following packages were installed and are no longer
required:
  gstreamer1.0-nice gstreamer1.0-plugins-bad gstreamer1.0-
plugins-good gstreamer1.0-x libbs2b0
```

The Snap version of the Dolphin application can be used on any Linux distribution that has Snap support.

Enable Snaps and Install a Dolphin

Snaps applications are packaged with dependencies to run on all popular Linux distributions from a single build. They update automatically and roll back gracefully.

Snaps are can installable from the Snap Store, an app store with an audience of millions.

Enable snapd in Terminal

Snap can install from the command line. Open the Konsole terminal window and enter the following:

```
$ sudo apt update
$ sudo apt install snapd
```

To install Dolphin, use the following command:

```
$ sudo snap install Dolphin
```

```
username@username-virtualbox:~$ sudo snap install Dolphin
Dolphin 21.08.3 from KDE* installed
```

It is a multi-document, multi-view text editor by KDE. It features code folding, syntax highlighting, dynamic word wrap, an embedded console, an extensive plugin interface, and preliminary scripting support.

Installing Dolphin from Ubuntu Repositories

Installing Dolphin from repositories is relatively straightforward and takes only a few minutes to complete.

Open a terminal using a keyboard shortcut, i.e., CTRL+ALT+T, and execute the below to update packages.

```
$ sudo apt update && sudo apt upgrade
```

```
username@username-virtualbox:~$ sudo apt install snapd
[sudo] password for username:
Reading package lists... Done
Building dependency tree          Done
Reading state information... Done
snapd is already the new version (2.51.1+20.04ubuntu2).
snapd set to manually installed.
Starting pkgProblemResolver with broken count: 0
Starting 2 pkgProblemResolver with broken count: 0
Done
The following packages were installed and are no longer
required:
  gstreamer1.0-nice gstreamer1.0-plugins-bad gstreamer1.0-
plugins-good gstreamer1.0-x libbs2b0
```

Now execute the given command to install the Dolphin package.

```
$ sudo apt install Dolphin
```

```
username@username-virtualbox:~$ sudo apt  install  Dolphin
[sudo] password for username:
Reading package lists... Done
Building dependency tree
Reading state information... Done
Dolphin is already the newest version (4:21.12.1-0xneon+20.
04+focal+release+build45).
Starting pkgProblemResolver with broken count: 0
Starting 2 pkgProblemResolver with broken count: 0
Done
The following packages were installed and are no longer
required:
  gstreamer1.0-nice gstreamer1.0-plugins-bad gstreamer1.0-
plugins-good gstreamer1.0-x
```

```
   libde265-0 libfarstream-0.2-5 libfluidsynth2 libgadu3
libgssdp-1.2-0
   libgstreamer-plugins-bad1.0-0 libgstreamer-plugins-
good1.0-0 libgupnp-1.2-0
   libgupnp-igd-1.0-4 libinstpatch-1.0-2 libmeanwhile1
libmjpegutils-2.1-0 libmms0 libmodplug1
   libmpeg2encpp-2.1-0 libmplex2-2.1-0 libnice10 libofa0
libprotobuf-c1 libpurple-bin
   libpurple0 libsoundtouch1 libspandsp2 libsrtp2-1
libusrsctp1 libv4l-0 libv4lconvert0
   libvo-aacenc0 libvo-amrwbenc0 libwildmidi2 libzbar0
libzephyr4 pidgin-data
   timgm6mb-soundfont
Use 'sudo apt autoremove' to remove them.
0 upgraded, 0 new installed, 0 to remove and 53 not
upgraded.
```

Features:

- Breadcrumb navigation bar

- Three view modes, i.e., Icons, Details, and Compact

- File Previews

- Split views used for copying and moving files

- Network transparency

- Undo/Redo functional

- Tab navigation

- Renaming of a variable number

- Baloo integration, which includes:

- File search

- Rating, Tagging, and commenting files

- Places bar, which integrates with the Kickoff launcher menu's "Computer" tab

- Grouping and sorting of files by name, size, type, and others

The first screen of Dolphin is given below,

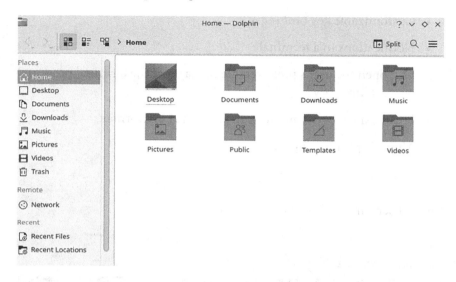

Dolphin window.

KONSOLE APPLICATION

It is a free and open source terminal emulator of KDE Applications and ships with the KDE desktop environment. Lars Doelle originally wrote Konsole. It is licensed under the GPL-2.0-or-later and the GNU Free Documentation License.

KDE applications, including Dolphin, Kate, KDevelop, Kile, Konversation, Konqueror, and Krusader, use Konsole to provide embedded terminal functionality via Kpart.

Features:

- Built-in support for bidirectional text display.

- Tabbed terminals

- Translucent backgrounds

- Split-view mode

- Directory and SSH bookmarking

- Customizable color schemes

- Incremental search

- Customizable key bindings

- Notifications in a terminal

- Can open the user's preferred file manager at the terminal program's current directory

- It can export of output in plain text or HTML format

- Multiple profile support

- Text reflow

The first screen of Konsole is given below,

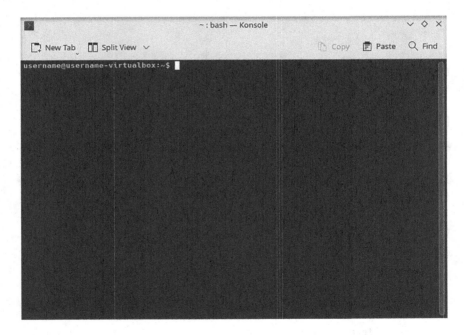

Konsole window.

A SIMPLE IMAGE VIEWER – GWENVIEW

Gwenview was available for KE 3. It was released in the KDE SC 4 with a user interface, making it more suitable for quickly browsing through the collection of images. It also provided a full-screen interface to display images as a slide show. It was ported to KDE Frameworks 5 and released as KDE Applications.

Gwenview is a fast and easy-to-use image viewer by KDE, ideal for browsing and displaying a collection of images, and is released as part of the KDE Applications bundle.

Installing Gwenview as a Snap Package

A snap package is a universal Linux package that you can enjoy irrespective of the distro. It is a self-contained software package that includes all dependencies needed to run the application.

If the snapd package is not installed, you can install it by running the following command:

```
$ sudo apt install snapd
```

```
username@username-virtualbox:~$ sudo apt install snapd
[sudo] password for username:
Reading package lists... Done
Building dependency tree      Done
Reading state information... Done
snapd is already the new version (2.51.1+20.04ubuntu2).
snapd set to manually installed.
Starting pkgProblemResolver with broken count: 0
Starting 2 pkgProblemResolver with broken count: 0
Done
The following packages were installed and are no longer
required:
  gstreamer1.0-nice gstreamer1.0-plugins-bad gstreamer1.0-
plugins-good gstreamer1.0-x libbs2b0
```

The Snap version of the **gwenview** application can be used on any Linux distribution that has Snap support.

Enable Snaps and Install a Gwenview

Snaps applications are packaged with dependencies to run on all popular Linux distributions from a single build. They update automatically and roll back gracefully.

Snaps are can installable from the Snap Store, an app store with an audience of millions.

Enable snapd in Terminal

Snap can install from the command line. Open the Konsole terminal window and enter the following:

```
$ sudo apt update
$ sudo apt install snapd
```

To install **gwenview**, use the following command:

```
$ sudo snap install gwenview
```

```
username@username-virtualbox:~$ sudo snap install gwenview
gwenview 21.08.3 from KDE* installed
```

It is a multi-document, multi-view text editor by KDE. It features code folding, syntax highlighting, dynamic word wrap, an embedded console, an extensive plugin interface, and preliminary scripting support.

Installing Gwenview from Ubuntu Repositories

Installing **gwenview** from repositories is relatively straightforward and takes only a few minutes to complete.

Open a terminal using a keyboard shortcut, i.e., CTRL+ALT+T, and execute the below to update packages.

```
$ sudo apt update && sudo apt upgrade
```

```
username@username-virtualbox:~$ sudo apt install snapd
[sudo] password for username:
Reading package lists... Done
Building dependency tree      Done
Reading state information... Done
snapd is already the new version (2.51.1+20.04ubuntu2).
snapd set to manually installed.
Starting pkgProblemResolver with broken count: 0
Starting 2 pkgProblemResolver with broken count: 0
Done
The following packages were installed and are no longer
required:
   gstreamer1.0-nice gstreamer1.0-plugins-bad gstreamer1.0-
plugins-good gstreamer1.0-x libbs2b0
```

Now execute the given command to install the gwenview package.

```
$ sudo apt install gwenview
```

```
seurname@username-virtualbox:~$ sudo apt install gwenview
[sudo] password for username:
Reading package lists... Done
Building dependency tree
Reading state information... Done
Starting pkgProblemResolver with broken count: 0
Starting 2 pkgProblemResolver with broken count: 0
Done
The following packages were installed and are no longer
required:0 upgraded, 0 newly installed, 0 to remove and 53
not upgraded.
```

Features:

- It supports simple image manipulations: rotate, mirror, flip, and resize.

- It supports file management actions such as copy, moves, deletes, and others.

- It can function on both as a standalone application and an embedded viewer in the Konqueror web browser.

- It can be extended using KIPI plugins.

Significant features include:

- Directory browser

- Raster images include but are not limited to BMP, PNG, JPEG, GIF, MNG, TIFF, PSD, SVG, RAW, and video support

- Easy to use interface

- Metadata comment editor

- Thumbnail image view of the current directory

- Import images from external storage

- Use of KIPI plugins for manipulating images

- It attempts filtering based on file type, file name pattern, and date

- Share images to social networking sites

The first screen of Gwenview is given below:

Gwenview Application window.

K3b APPLICATION

It is a CD and DVD application by KDE for Unix operating systems. It provides a GUI to perform most CD/DVD burning tasks like creating an audio CD from a set of files or copying a CD/DVD and more advanced tasks such as burning eMoviX CD/DVDs. It can also perform direct disc-to-disc copies. The program has many default settings that more experienced users can customize. The actual disc recording is done by the command line utilities cdrecord or cdrkit, cdrdao, and growisofs. K3b features a built-in DVD ripper.

K3b is written in the C++ language and uses the Qt toolkit. Its release was under the GNU General Public License. K3 b is free software.

The first KDE Platform 4 version of K3b was released on April 22, 2009.

K3b is one of the mainstays of the KDE desktop software project started in 1998.

Installing K3b from Ubuntu Repositories

Installing **K3b** from repositories is relatively straightforward and takes only a few minutes to complete.

Open a terminal using a keyboard shortcut, i.e., CTRL+ALT+T, and execute the below to update packages.

```
$ sudo apt update && sudo apt upgrade
```

```
username@username-virtualbox:~$ sudo apt install snapd
[sudo] password for username:
Reading package lists... Done
Building dependency tree    Done
Reading state information... Done
snapd is already the new version (2.51.1+20.04ubuntu2).
snapd set to manually installed.
Starting pkgProblemResolver with broken count: 0
Starting 2 pkgProblemResolver with broken count: 0
Done
The following packages were installed and are no longer
required:
  gstreamer1.0-nice gstreamer1.0-plugins-bad gstreamer1.0-
plugins-good gstreamer1.0-x libbs2b0
```

Now execute the given command to install the **K3b** package.

```
$ sudo apt install K3b
```

```
username@username-virtualbox:~$ sudo apt install k3b
Reading package lists... Done
Building dependency tree
Reading state information... Done
Starting pkgProblemResolver with broken count: 0
Starting 2 pkgProblemResolver with broken count: 0
Done
The following packages were installed and are no longer
required:
  autoconf automake autotools-dev cpp-8 dvdauthor dvgrab
ffmpeg frei0r-plugins gcc gcc-8
```

Some of the main features include:

- Data CD/DVD burning

- Audio CD burning

- CD-Text support

- Support the Blu-ray/DVD-R/DVD+R/DVD-RW/DVD+RW

- Support CD-R/CD-RW

- Mixed Mode and Multisession CD

- Video CD/Video DVD authoring

- eMovix CD/eMovix DVD

- Disk-to-disk CD and DVD copying

- Erasing CD-RW/DVD-RW/DVD+RW

- ISO image support

- Ripping Audio CDs, Video CDs, Video DVDs

The first screen of K3b is given below:

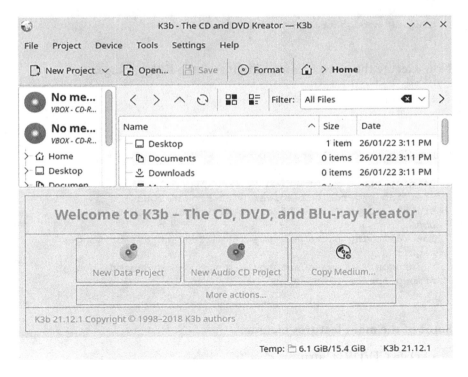

K3b Application window.

KMAIL APPLICATION

It is a mail client that integrates with widely used email providers such as Gmail. It provides various tools and features to maximize productivity and makes working with large email accounts straightforward and quick. It supports many email protocols – POP3, IMAP, Microsoft Exchange (EWS), and more.

Installing KMail from Ubuntu Repositories

Installing **KMail** from repositories is relatively straightforward and takes only a few minutes to complete.

Open a terminal using a keyboard shortcut, i.e., CTRL+ALT+T, and execute the below to update packages.

```
$ sudo apt update && sudo apt upgrade
```

```
username@username-virtualbox:~$ sudo apt install
snapd
[sudo] password for username:
Reading package lists... Done
Building dependency tree      Done
Reading state information... Done
snapd is already the new version
(2.51.1+20.04ubuntu2).
snapd set to manually installed.
Starting pkgProblemResolver with broken count: 0
Starting 2 pkgProblemResolver with broken count: 0
Done
The following packages were installed and are no
longer required:
  gstreamer1.0-nice gstreamer1.0-plugins-bad
gstreamer1.0-plugins-good gstreamer1.0-x libbs2b0
```

Now execute the given command to install the **KMail** package.

```
$ sudo apt install Kmail
```

```
username@username-virtualbox:~$ sudo apt install kmail
Reading package lists... Done
Building dependency tree
```

```
Reading state information... Done
Starting pkgProblemResolver with broken count: 0
Starting 2 pkgProblemResolver with broken count: 0
Done
The following packages were installed and are no longer
required:
  autoconf automake autotools-dev cpp-8 dvdauthor dvgrab
ffmpeg frei0r-plugins gcc gcc-8
```

Features:

- **Secure:** KMail has specific default settings to protect your privacy, great end-to-end encryption support, and spam detection.

- **Powerful:** Features include:

  1. Offline support

  2. Multiple sender identities

  3. Multi-language support

  4. Powerful filtering

  5. Searching and tagging functionality

  6. Mailing list management

  7. Very flexible configuration

- **Integrated:** Meeting invitations can be easily added as events into KOrganizer, address auto-completion, avatars, and crypto preferences are loaded from KAddressBook.

- **Standard Compliant:** Supports standard mail protocols, push email, server-side filtering, and inline OpenPGP, PGP/MIME, and S/MIME.

The first screen of KMail is given below:

KMail Application window.

KORGANIZER APPLICATION

It is the calendar and scheduling component of Kontact that an integrated personal information manager from KDE.

You can download Korgainzer from the KDE Application Discover. You need to search for an application it will show some result as given below:

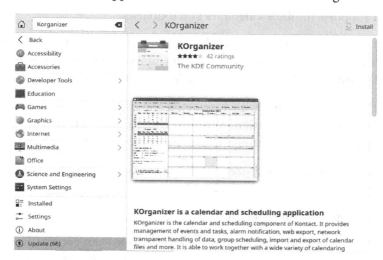

Korganizer Application.

Click on the install button.

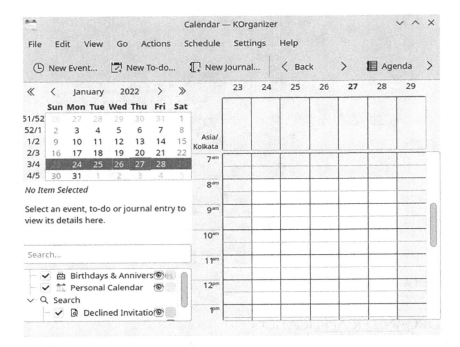

Korganizer Application window.

Features:

- It supports multiple calendars and todo lists.

- It can transparently merge calendar data from different files or other calendar data sources, such as calendars. They can be activated, deactivated, added, and removed from the GUI.

- It is fully integrated with Kontact, a complete personal information management application. Within Kontact, some other features are available, like converting mails to events or todos by drag and drop.

- Storage model. KOrganizer has a persistent calendar. The user doesn't have to load or save the calendar. Changes are immediately saved to disk.

- It supports unlimited undo and redo.

- Todos are shown in the weekday views. Todos can convert to events by dragging them from the todo list and dropping them on the agenda view.

- Attachments for events and todos. References to web pages, local files, or emails can be attached to events and todos. The linked data can easily be accessed by a single click from the event and todo views and the editors' summary view.

- Quick to do an entry. A particular input field allows quickly creating a todo without opening an editor. It is convenient for creating multiple todos in a row.

- Print support. Calendars can be printed using various styles. Printing also supports colors and overlapping events.

- KMail supports the direct transfer of invitations and other calendar attachments to KOrganizer.

PARLEY APPLICATION

Parley is a vocabulary trainer. It helps you memorize your vocabulary, for example, when you are trying to learn a foreign language. It supports many language-specific features but can also be used for other learning tasks. It uses the spaced repetition method, which makes learning optimal.

Installing Parley as a Snap Package

A snap package is a universal Linux package that you can enjoy irrespective of the distro. It is a self-contained software package that includes all dependencies needed to run the application.

If the snapd package is not installed, you can install it by running the following command:

```
$ sudo apt install snapd
```

```
username@username-virtualbox:~$ sudo apt install snapd
[sudo] password for username:
Reading package lists... Done
Building dependency tree      Done
Reading state information... Done
snapd is already the new version (2.51.1+20.04ubuntu2).
snapd set to manually installed.
Starting pkgProblemResolver with broken count: 0
Starting 2 pkgProblemResolver with broken count: 0
Done
The following packages were  installed and are no longer
required:
  gstreamer1.0-nice gstreamer1.0-plugins-bad gstreamer1.0-
plugins-good gstreamer1.0-x libbs2b0
```

The Snap version of the **parley application** can be used on any Linux distribution that has Snap support.

Enable Snaps and Install a Parley

Snaps applications are packaged with dependencies to run on all popular Linux distributions from a single build. They update automatically and roll back gracefully.

Snaps are can installable from the Snap Store, an app store with an audience of millions.

Enable snapd in Terminal

Snap can install from the command line. Open the Konsole terminal window and enter the following:

```
$ sudo apt update
$ sudo apt install snapd
```

To install **parley**, use the following command:

```
$ sudo snap install parley
```

```
username@username-virtualbox:~$ sudo snap install parley
parley  21.08.3 from KDE* installed
```

It is a multi-document, multi-view text editor by KDE. It features code folding, syntax highlighting, dynamic word wrap, an embedded console, an extensive plugin interface, and preliminary scripting support.

Installing Parley from Ubuntu Repositories

Installing parley from repositories is relatively straightforward and takes only a few minutes to complete.

Open a terminal using a keyboard shortcut, i.e., CTRL+ALT+T, and execute the below to update packages.

```
$ sudo apt update && sudo apt upgrade
```

```
username@username-virtualbox:~$ sudo apt install snapd
[sudo] password for username:
Reading package lists... Done
Building dependency tree      Done
Reading state information... Done
snapd is already the new version (2.51.1+20.04ubuntu2).
snapd set to manually installed.
Starting pkgProblemResolver with broken count: 0
Starting 2 pkgProblemResolver with broken count: 0
Done
The following packages were installed and are no longer
required:
  gstreamer1.0-nice gstreamer1.0-plugins-bad gstreamer1.0-
plugins-good gstreamer1.0-x libbs2b0
```

Now execute the given command to install the **parley** package.

```
$ sudo apt install parley
```

```
username@username-virtualbox:~$ sudo apt install parley
Reading package lists... Done
Building dependency tree
Reading state information... Done
Starting pkgProblemResolver with broken count: 0
Starting 2 pkgProblemResolver with broken count: 0
Done
The following packages were installed and are no longer
required:
  autoconf automake autotools-dev cpp-8 dvdauthor dvgrab
ffmpeg frei0r-plugins gcc gcc-8
```

Features:

- FlashCards
- Mixed letters
- Multiple choice
- Written
- Language-specific pieces of training: article, comparison forms, conjugations, synonyms/antonyms/paraphrases
- Different test types

- Written tests (including clever correction mechanisms)

- Article training

- Comparison forms such as adjectives, conjugations, and adverbs

- Synonym, antonym, paraphrase

- Easy lesson management

- Fast test setup with all options in a dialog

- More than two languages, for example, English, Chinese Traditional, and Chinese Simplified

- Find words

- Premade vocabulary files

- Share and download vocabulary using Get Hot New Stuff

- Open XML file format that can be edited by hand and is easily usable with scripts

The first screen of Parley is given below:

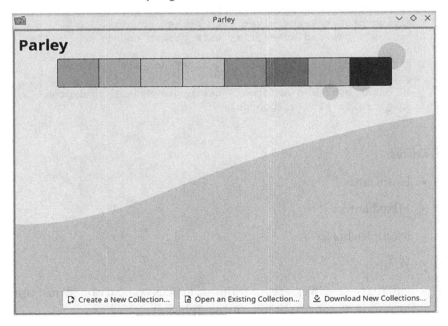

Parley Application window.

BLINKEN APPLICATION

It is based on an electronic game that challenges players to remember sequences of increasing length. There are four different color buttons, each one with its distinctive sound. These buttons light up randomly, creating the series that the player must recall. If the player successfully remembers the sequence of lights correctly, they move to the next stage, where the same sequence with an extra step is presented. If they are not correct, the game is lost, and the player starts again from the beginning. The goal is to get each step in the sequence is worth one point, so the correct entry of a sequence of 8 lights is worth 8 points on the high-score table.

Installing Blinken as a Snap Package

A snap package is a universal Linux package that you can enjoy irrespective of the distro. It is a self-contained software package that includes all dependencies needed to run the application.

If the snapd package is not installed, you can install it by running the following command:

```
$ sudo apt install snapd
```

```
username@username-virtualbox:~$ sudo apt install snapd
[sudo] password for username:
Reading package lists... Done
Building dependency tree       Done
Reading state information... Done
snapd is already the new version (2.51.1+20.04ubuntu2).
snapd set to manually installed.
Starting pkgProblemResolver with broken count: 0
Starting 2 pkgProblemResolver with broken count: 0
Done
The following packages were installed and are no longer
required:
  gstreamer1.0-nice gstreamer1.0-plugins-bad gstreamer1.0-
plugins-good gstreamer1.0-x libbs2b0
```

The Snap version of the blinken application can be used on any Linux distribution that has Snap support.

Enable Snaps and Install a Blinken

Snaps applications are packaged with dependencies to run on all popular Linux distributions from a single build. They update automatically and roll back gracefully.

Snaps are can installable from the Snap Store, an app store with an audience of millions.

Enable snapd in Terminal

Snap can install from the command line. Open the Konsole terminal window and enter the following:

```
$ sudo apt update
$ sudo apt install snapd
```

To install blinken, use the following command:

```
$ sudo snap install blinken
```

```
username@username-virtualbox:~$ sudo snap install blinken
blinken 21.08.3 from KDE* installed
```

It is a multi-document, multi-view text editor by KDE. It features code folding, syntax highlighting, dynamic word wrap, an embedded console, an extensive plugin interface, and preliminary scripting support.

Installing Blinken from Ubuntu Repositories

Installing blinken from repositories is relatively straightforward and takes only a few minutes to complete.

Open a terminal using a keyboard shortcut, i.e., CTRL+ALT+T, and execute the below to update packages.

```
$ sudo apt update && sudo apt upgrade
```

```
username@username-virtualbox:~$ sudo apt install snapd
[sudo] password for username:
Reading package lists... Done
Building dependency tree     Done
Reading state information... Done
snapd is already the new version (2.51.1+20.04ubuntu2).
snapd set to manually installed.
Starting pkgProblemResolver with broken count: 0
Starting 2 pkgProblemResolver with broken count: 0
Done
```

```
The following packages were installed and are no longer
required:
   gstreamer1.0-nice gstreamer1.0-plugins-bad gstreamer1.0-
plugins-good gstreamer1.0-x libbs2b0
```

Now execute the given command to install the blinken package.

```
$ sudo apt-get install blinken
```

```
username@username-virtualbox:~$ sudo apt-get install
blinken
Reading package lists... Done
Building dependency tree
Reading state information... Done
Starting pkgProblemResolver with broken count: 0
Starting 2 pkgProblemResolver with broken count: 0
Done
The following packages were installed and are no longer
required:
   autoconf automake autotools-dev cpp-8 dvdauthor dvgrab
ffmpeg frei0r-plugins gcc gcc-8
```

The first screen of Blinken is given below,

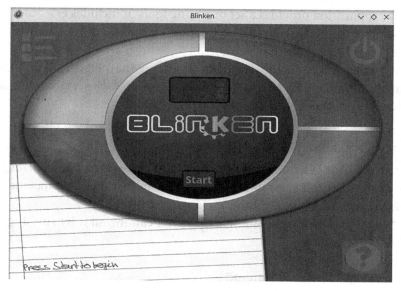

Blinken Application window.

PHOTO MANAGEMENT PROGRAM – digiKam APPLICATION

It is an open source digital photo management application that works well on Linux, Windows, and macOS. It gives a set of tools for importing, managing, editing, and sharing photos and raw files. You can use digiKam's import capabilities to quickly transfer photos, raw files, and videos instantly from camera and external storage devices. It allows you to configure import settings and rules that process and organize imported items on the fly.

It can organize photos, raw files, and videos into albums. The application features powerful tagging tools that allow you to assign tags, ratings, and labels to pictures and raw files. You can use filtering functionality to find items that match specific criteria.

It also has powerful searching capabilities that allow you to search the photo library by a wide range of criteria. You can search photos by rating, date, location, tags, labels, and even specific EXIF, IPTC, and XMP metadata. You can even combine other criteria for more advanced searches. It relies on the Exiv2 library to handle metadata tags.

It can handle raw files. The library is maintained and regularly updated to support the latest camera model and manage video files for cataloging purposes. The application uses the couple FFmpeg and QtAv libraries to extract metadata and play media.

The application provides a set of editing tools. It includes essential tools for adjusting colors, cropping, sharpening, advanced curves adjustment, panorama stitching, and much more.

It can be implemented via tools based on the plugin's mechanism. Plugins can import and export contents to remote web services, add new features to edit images, and batch process photos.

Installing digiKam as a Snap Package

A snap package is a universal Linux package that you can enjoy irrespective of the distro. It is a self-contained software package that includes all dependencies needed to run the application.

If the snapd package is not installed, you can install it by running the following command:

```
$ sudo apt install snapd
```

```
username@username-virtualbox:~$ sudo apt install snapd
[sudo] password for username:
Reading package lists... Done
Building dependency tree      Done
Reading state information... Done
snapd is already the new version (2.51.1+20.04ubuntu2).
snapd set to manually installed.
Starting pkgProblemResolver with broken count: 0
Starting 2 pkgProblemResolver with broken count: 0
Done
The following packages were installed and are no longer
required:
  gstreamer1.0-nice gstreamer1.0-plugins-bad gstreamer1.0-
plugins-good gstreamer1.0-x libbs2b0
```

The Snap version of the digiKam application can be used on any Linux
distribution that has Snap support.

Enable Snaps and Install a digiKam

Snaps applications are packaged with dependencies to run on all popular
Linux distributions from a single build. They update automatically and
roll back gracefully.

Snaps are can installable from the Snap Store, an app store with an audience of millions.

Enable snapd in Terminal

Snap can install from the command line. Open the Konsole terminal window and enter the following:

```
$ sudo apt update
$ sudo apt install snapd
```

To install digiKam, use the following command:

```
$ sudo snap install digikam
```

```
username@username-virtualbox:~$ sudo snap install digikam
digikam 21.08.3 from KDE* installed
```

It is a multi-document, multi-view text editor by KDE. It features code folding, syntax highlighting, dynamic word wrap, an embedded console, an extensive plugin interface, and preliminary scripting support.

Installing digiKam from Ubuntu Repositories

Installing digiKam from repositories is relatively straightforward and takes only a few minutes to complete.

Open a terminal using a keyboard shortcut, i.e., CTRL+ALT+T, and execute the below to update packages.

```
$ sudo apt update && sudo apt upgrade
```

```
username@username-virtualbox:~$ sudo apt install snapd
[sudo] password for username:
Reading package lists... Done
Building dependency tree       Done
Reading state information... Done
snapd is already the new version (2.51.1+20.04ubuntu2).
snapd set to manually installed.
Starting pkgProblemResolver with broken count: 0
Starting 2 pkgProblemResolver with broken count: 0
Done
The following packages were installed and are no longer
required:
   gstreamer1.0-nice gstreamer1.0-plugins-bad gstreamer1.0-
plugins-good gstreamer1.0-x libbs2b0
```

Now execute the given command to install the digiKam package.

```
$ sudo apt-get install digikam
```

```
username@username-virtualbox:~$ sudo apt-get install
digikam
Reading package lists... Done
Building dependency tree
Reading state information... Done
Starting pkgProblemResolver with broken count: 0
Starting 2 pkgProblemResolver with broken count: 0
Done
The following packages were installed and are no longer
required:
   autoconf automake autotools-dev cpp-8 dvdauthor dvgrab
ffmpeg frei0r-plugins gcc gcc-8
```

Features:

- Support for 900+ RAW format pictures

- Organization of photos in albums and sub-albums

- Support for Exif, Iptc, Xmp, Maker notes

- Support for filtering and sorting albums

- SQLite or Mysql storage for the album contents

- Import from 1100+ digital camera devices

- Light Table to compare photo side by side

- Extended features using extra tools

The first screen of digiKam is given below:

digiKam Application window.

KONQUEROR APPLICATION

Konqueror is KDE's Webbrowser and swiss-army-knife for file management and previewing.

Installing Konqueror from Ubuntu Repositories

Installing konqueror from repositories is relatively straightforward and takes only a few minutes to complete.

Open a terminal using a keyboard shortcut, i.e., CTRL+ALT+T, and execute the below to update packages.

```
$ sudo apt update && sudo apt upgrade
```

```
username@username-virtualbox:~$ sudo apt install snapd
Reading package lists... Done
Building dependency tree       Done
Reading state information... Done
snapd is already the new version (2.51.1+20.04ubuntu2).
snapd set to manually installed.
Starting pkgProblemResolver with broken count: 0
Starting 2 pkgProblemResolver with broken count: 0
Done
The following packages were installed and are no longer
required:
  gstreamer1.0-nice gstreamer1.0-plugins-bad gstreamer1.0-
plugins-good gstreamer1.0-x libbs2b0
```

Now execute the given command to install the konqueror package.

```
$ sudo apt-get install konqueror
```

```
username@username-virtualbox:~$ sudo apt-get install
konqueror
Reading package lists... Done
Building dependency tree
Reading state information... Done
Starting pkgProblemResolver with broken count: 0
Starting 2 pkgProblemResolver with broken count: 0
Done
The following packages were installed and are no longer
required:
  autoconf automake autotools-dev cpp-8 dvdauthor dvgrab
ffmpeg frei0r-plugins gcc gcc-8
```

Features:

- Web browsing using KHTML or KDEWebKit as rendering engines.

- File management using most of Dolphin's features, including version-control, service menus, and the basic UI.

- File management on FTP and sftp servers.

- Full-featured FTP-client.

- Embedded applications to preview files, for example, Okular and Calligra for documents, Gwenview for pictures, KTextEditor for text files.

- Different kinds of plugins: Service-menus, KParts embedded applications, KIO like accessing files using particular protocols like HTTP or FTP, and KPart-plugins like AdBlocker.

The first screen of konqueror is given below:

konqueror Application window.

COLOR CHOOSER AND PALETTE EDITOR

KColorChooser is a color palette used to mix colors and create custom color palettes. It can obtain the color of the pixel on the screen. Several typical color palettes are included, such as the standard Web colors and the Oxygen color scheme.

KColorChooser (Color Chooser) is a graphics application developed by KDE. It is included in the kdegraphics package. The program enables users to pick any color or color palette from the screen. Colors that are picked up may be saved or added into Custom Colors.

KColorChooser (Color Chooser) features a light gray user interface. The upper left corner features the color picker tool. The upper left panel displays the color gradation window. It shows a full spectrum of color. Besides, that is the full gradation of the selected color. For example, once the user selects the color blue from the spectrum, all the gradations of blue will be displayed on the larger window beside it. This gradation ranges from white to the lightest blue to the darkest shade of blue until black.

Installing kcolorchooser as a Snap Package

A snap package is a universal Linux package that you can enjoy irrespective of the distro. It is a self-contained software package that includes all dependencies needed to run the application.

If the snapd package is not installed, you can install it by running the following command:

```
$ sudo apt install snapd
```

```
username@username-virtualbox:~$ sudo apt install snapd
[sudo] password for username:
Reading package lists... Done
Building dependency tree      Done
Reading state information... Done
snapd is already the new version (2.51.1+20.04ubuntu2).
snapd set to manually installed.
Starting pkgProblemResolver with broken count: 0
Starting 2 pkgProblemResolver with broken count: 0
Done
The following packages were installed and are no longer
required:
  gstreamer1.0-nice gstreamer1.0-plugins-bad gstreamer1.0-
plugins-good gstreamer1.0-x libbs2b0
```

The Snap version of the kcolorchooser application can be used on any Linux distribution that has Snap support.

Enable Snaps and Install a kcolorchooser

Snaps applications are packaged with dependencies to run on all popular Linux distributions from a single build. They update automatically and roll back gracefully.

Snaps are can installable from the Snap Store, an app store with an audience of millions.

Enable snapd in Terminal

Snap can install from the command line. Open the Konsole terminal window and enter the following:

```
$ sudo apt update
$ sudo apt install snapd
```

To install kcolorchooser, use the following command:

```
$ sudo snap install kcolorchooser
```

```
username@username-virtualbox:~$ sudo snap install
kcolorchooser
kcolorchooser 21.08.3 from KDE* installed
```

It is a multi-document, multi-view text editor by KDE. It features code folding, syntax highlighting, dynamic word wrap, an embedded console, an extensive plugin interface, and preliminary scripting support.

Installing kcolorchooser from Ubuntu Repositories

Installing kcolorchooser from repositories is relatively straightforward and takes only a few minutes to complete.

Open a terminal using a keyboard shortcut, i.e., CTRL+ALT+T, and execute the below to update packages.

```
$ sudo apt update && sudo apt upgrade
```

```
username@username-virtualbox:~$ sudo apt install snapd
[sudo] password for username:
Reading package lists... Done
Building dependency tree       Done
Reading state information... Done
snapd is already the new version (2.51.1+20.04ubuntu2).
snapd set to manually installed.
Starting pkgProblemResolver with broken count: 0
Starting 2 pkgProblemResolver with broken count: 0
Done
The following packages were installed and are no longer
required:
  gstreamer1.0-nice gstreamer1.0-plugins-bad gstreamer1.0-
plugins-good gstreamer1.0-x libbs2b0
```

Now execute the given command to install the kcolorchooser package.

```
$ sudo apt-get install kcolorchooser
```

```
username@username-virtualbox:~$ sudo apt-get install
kcolorchooser
Reading package lists... Done
Building dependency tree
Reading state information... Done
Starting pkgProblemResolver with broken count: 0
Starting 2 pkgProblemResolver with broken count: 0
Done
The following packages were installed and are no longer
required:
   autoconf automake autotools-dev cpp-8 dvdauthor dvgrab
ffmpeg frei0r-plugins gcc gcc-8
```

Users can also choose among the preinstalled color collection by clicking on the drop-down list. Below the color, the collection picker is a window displaying the different colors inside the group. Users can also choose exactly the HTML code for the color they prefer. Using the HTML input box and preview button on the lower right panel is possible. Once color is selected, users may change some configurations, including Hue, Saturation, and Value. Users can also adjust the color by toggling the Red, Green, and Blue values.

The first screen of kcolorchooser is given below:

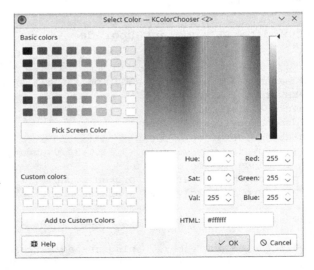

kcolorchooser Application window.

KBACKUP APPLICATION

Kbackup is an application that allows you to back up your data in a simple, user-friendly way.

Installing KBackup from Ubuntu Repositories

Installing kbackup from repositories is relatively straightforward and takes only a few minutes to complete.

Open a terminal using a keyboard shortcut, i.e., CTRL+ALT+T, and execute the below to update packages.

```
$ sudo apt update && sudo apt upgrade
```

```
username@username-virtualbox:~$ sudo apt install snapd
[sudo] password for username:
Reading package lists... Done
Building dependency tree     Done
Reading state information... Done
snapd is already the new version (2.51.1+20.04ubuntu2).
snapd set to manually installed.
Starting pkgProblemResolver with broken count: 0
Starting 2 pkgProblemResolver with broken count: 0
Done
The following packages were  installed and are no longer
required:
  gstreamer1.0-nice gstreamer1.0-plugins-bad gstreamer1.0-
plugins-good gstreamer1.0-x libbs2b0
```

Now execute the given command to install the kbackup package.

```
$ sudo apt-get install kbackup
```

```
username@username-virtualbox:~$ sudo apt-get install
kbackup
Reading package lists... Done
Building dependency tree
Reading state information... Done
Starting pkgProblemResolver with broken count: 0
Starting 2 pkgProblemResolver with broken count: 0
Done
The following packages were installed and are no longer
required:
  autoconf automake autotools-dev cpp-8 dvdauthor dvgrab
ffmpeg frei0r-plugins gcc gcc-8
```

Features:

- It is using profile files with definitions for both folders and files to be included or excluded from the backup.

- The backup target can either be a locally mounted device, like a ZIP drive, USB stick, etc., or any remote URL.

- Supports automated backups without using a graphical user interface.

The first screen of backup is given below,

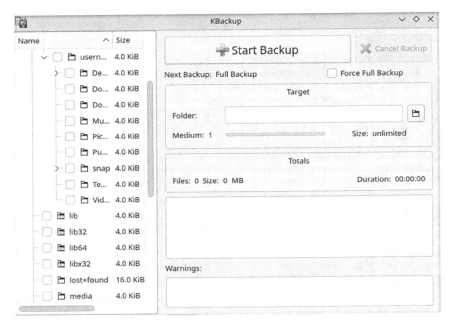

kbackup Application window.

KNOTES APPLICATION

It is an application that allows you to write the computer equivalent of sticky notes.

The notes are saved when you exit the program, and they display when you open the program. It is free and open source software.

Installing KNotes from Ubuntu Repositories

Installing knotes from repositories is relatively straightforward and takes only a few minutes to complete.

Open a terminal using a keyboard shortcut, i.e., CTRL+ALT+T, and execute the below to update packages.

```
$ sudo apt update && sudo apt upgrade
```

```
username@username-virtualbox:~$ sudo apt install snapd
[sudo] password for username:
Reading package lists... Done
Building dependency tree      Done
Reading state information... Done
snapd is already the new version (2.51.1+20.04ubuntu2).
snapd set to manually installed.
Starting pkgProblemResolver with broken count: 0
Starting 2 pkgProblemResolver with broken count: 0
Done
The following packages were installed and are no longer
required:
  gstreamer1.0-nice gstreamer1.0-plugins-bad gstreamer1.0-
plugins-good gstreamer1.0-x libbs2b0
```

Now execute the given command to install the knotes package.

```
$ sudo apt-get install knotes
```

```
username@username-virtualbox:~$ sudo apt-get install knotes
Reading package lists... Done
Building dependency tree
Reading state information... Done
Starting pkgProblemResolver with broken count: 0
Starting 2 pkgProblemResolver with broken count: 0
Done
The following packages were  installed and are no longer
required:
  autoconf automake autotools-dev cpp-8 dvdauthor dvgrab
ffmpeg frei0r-plugins gcc gcc-8
```

Features:

- You can write notes of your choice of font and background color. Display features such as color and font may be customized for each note. You may also customize the defaults.

- It can generate a new note from the clipboard's contents or a text file.

- It uses drag and drop features to email your notes.

- It can drag into the Calendar to book a time slot.

- Even notes can print.

- Keyboard shortcuts are available.

The first screen knotes of is given below:

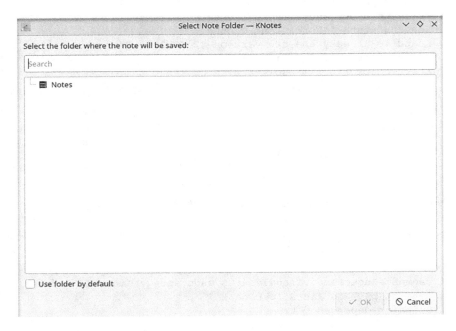

knotes Application window.

KMOUSETOOL APPLICATION

It clicks the mouse whenever the cursor pauses.

Installing KMouseTool as a Snap Package

A snap package is a universal Linux package that you can enjoy irrespective of the distro. It is a self-contained software package that includes all dependencies needed to run the application.

If the snapd package is not installed, you can install it by running the following command:

```
$ sudo apt install snapd
```

```
username@username-virtualbox:~$ sudo apt install snapd
[sudo] password for username:
Reading package lists... Done
Building dependency tree       Done
Reading state information... Done
snapd is already the new version (2.51.1+20.04ubuntu2).
snapd set to manually installed.
Starting pkgProblemResolver with broken count: 0
Starting 2 pkgProblemResolver with broken count: 0
Done
The following packages were installed and are no longer
required:
  gstreamer1.0-nice gstreamer1.0-plugins-bad gstreamer1.0-
plugins-good gstreamer1.0-x libbs2b0
```

The Snap version of the kmousetool application can be used on any Linux distribution that has Snap support.

Enable Snaps and Install a KMouseTool

Snaps applications are packaged with dependencies to run on all popular Linux distributions from a single build. They update automatically and roll back gracefully.

Snaps are can installable from the Snap Store, an app store with an audience of millions.

Enable snapd in Terminal

Snap can install from the command line. Open the Konsole terminal window and enter the following:

```
$ sudo apt update
$ sudo apt install snapd
```

To install kmousetool, use the following command:

```
$ sudo snap install kmousetool
```

```
username@username-virtualbox:~$ sudo snap install
kmousetool  --candidate
kcolorchooser (candidate) 21.08.3 from KDE* installed
```

It is a multi-document, multi-view text editor by KDE. It features code folding, syntax highlighting, dynamic word wrap, an embedded console, an extensive plugin interface, and preliminary scripting support.

Installing KMouseTool from Ubuntu Repositories

Installing kmousetool from repositories is relatively straightforward and takes only a few minutes to complete.

Open a terminal using a keyboard shortcut, i.e., CTRL+ALT+T, and execute the below to update packages.

```
$ sudo apt update && sudo apt upgrade
```

```
username@username-virtualbox:~$ sudo apt install snapd
[sudo] password for username:
Reading package lists... Done
Building dependency tree      Done
Reading state information... Done
snapd is already the new version (2.51.1+20.04ubuntu2).
snapd set to manually installed.
Starting pkgProblemResolver with broken count: 0
Starting 2 pkgProblemResolver with broken count: 0
Done
The following packages were  installed and are no longer
required:
  gstreamer1.0-nice gstreamer1.0-plugins-bad gstreamer1.0-
plugins-good gstreamer1.0-x libbs2b0
```

Now execute the given command to install the kmousetool package.

```
$ sudo apt-get install kmousetool
```

```
username@username-virtualbox:~$ sudo apt-get install
kmousetool
Reading package lists... Done
Building dependency tree
Reading state information... Done
Starting pkgProblemResolver with broken count: 0
Starting 2 pkgProblemResolver with broken count: 0
Done
The following packages were installed and are no longer
required:
  autoconf automake autotools-dev cpp-8 dvdauthor dvgrab
ffmpeg frei0r-plugins gcc gcc-8
```

The first screen kmousetool of is given below:

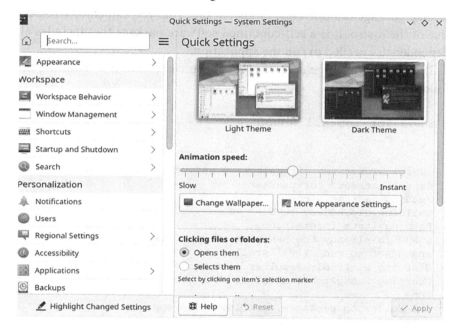

kmousetool Application window.

KBARCODE APPLICATION

It is a barcode and label printing application for KDE. It printed everything from simple business cards to complex labels with several barcodes (e.g., article descriptions). KBarcode comes with an easy-to-use setup wizard, WYSIWYG label designer, batch import of data for batch printing labels, hundreds of predefined labels, database management tools, and translations in various languages. It is printing more than 10,000 labels in one go. Data for printing can import from several different data sources, including SQL databases, CSV files, and the KDE address book.

It is a simple barcode generator. All major barcodes like EAN, UPC, CODE39, and ISBN are supported. Even complex 2D barcodes are supported using third-party tools. The generated barcodes can print or export into images in another application.

KTUBERLING APPLICATION

It is a game suitable for children and adults. It is a drawing toy for small children with several activities.

Installing KTuberling as a Snap Package

A snap package is a universal Linux package that you can enjoy irrespective of the distro. It is a self-contained software package that includes all dependencies needed to run the application.

If the snapd package is not installed, you can install it by running the following command:

```
$ sudo apt install snapd
```

```
username@username-virtualbox:~$ sudo apt install snapd
[sudo] password for username:
Reading package lists... Done
Building dependency tree      Done
Reading state information... Done
snapd is already the new version (2.51.1+20.04ubuntu2).
snapd set to manually installed.
Starting pkgProblemResolver with broken count: 0
Starting 2 pkgProblemResolver with broken count: 0
Done
The following packages were installed and are no longer
required:
   gstreamer1.0-nice gstreamer1.0-plugins-bad gstreamer1.0-
plugins-good gstreamer1.0-x libbs2b0
```

The Snap version of the ktuberling application can be used on any Linux distribution that has Snap support.

Enable Snaps and Install a KTuberling

Snaps applications are packaged with dependencies to run on all popular Linux distributions from a single build. They update automatically and roll back gracefully.

Snaps are can installable from the Snap Store, an app store with an audience of millions.

Enable snapd in Terminal

Snap can install from the command line. Open the Konsole terminal window and enter the following:

```
$ sudo apt update
$ sudo apt install snapd
```

To install ktuberling, use the following command:

```
$ sudo snap install ktuberling
```

```
username@username-virtualbox:~$ sudo snap install
ktuberling  --candidate
ktuberling  (candidate) 21.08.3 from KDE* installed
```

It is a multi-document, multi-view text editor by KDE. It features code folding, syntax highlighting, dynamic word wrap, an embedded console, an extensive plugin interface, and preliminary scripting support.

Installing KTuberling from Ubuntu Repositories

Installing ktuberling from repositories is relatively straightforward and takes only a few minutes to complete.

Open a terminal using a keyboard shortcut, i.e., CTRL+ALT+T, and execute the below to update packages.

```
$ sudo apt update && sudo apt upgrade
```

```
username@username-virtualbox:~$ sudo apt install snapd
[sudo] password for username:
Reading package lists... Done
Building dependency tree      Done
Reading state information... Done
snapd is already the new version (2.51.1+20.04ubuntu2).
snapd set to manually installed.
Starting pkgProblemResolver with broken count: 0
Starting 2 pkgProblemResolver with broken count: 0
Done
The following packages were installed and are no longer
required:
  gstreamer1.0-nice gstreamer1.0-plugins-bad gstreamer1.0-
plugins-good gstreamer1.0-x libbs2b0
```

Now execute the given command to install the ktuberling package.

```
$ sudo apt-get install ktuberling
```

```
username@username-virtualbox:~$ sudo apt-get install
ktuberling
Reading package lists... Done
Building dependency tree
Reading state information... Done
Starting pkgProblemResolver with broken count: 0
Starting 2 pkgProblemResolver with broken count: 0
Done
The following packages were installed and are no longer
required:
  autoconf automake autotools-dev cpp-8 dvdauthor dvgrab
ffmpeg frei0r-plugins gcc gcc-8
```

Features:

- It gives the potato a funny face, clothes, and other goodies.

- It builds a small town, complete with school, zoo, and fire department.

- It can create a fantastic moonscape with spaceships and aliens.

- It can speak the name of each object in several languages to assist in learning basic vocabulary. The package is part of the KDE games module.

The first screen ktuberling of is given below:

ktuberling Application window.

KPHOTOALBUM APPLICATION

It is an image viewer and organizer created by Jesper K. Pedersen. The philosophy behind its creation was that it is easy for users to annotate images and videos taken with a digital camera. Anyone can search for images based on annotations called categories, and use the results in various ways. It has features include slideshows, annotation, KIPI plugin support for manipulating images, and Boolean searches. It is previously known as KimDaBa.

Installing KPhotoAlbum from Ubuntu Repositories

Installing kphotoalbum from repositories is relatively straightforward and takes only a few minutes to complete.

Open a terminal using a keyboard shortcut, i.e., CTRL+ALT+T, and execute the below to update packages.

```
$ sudo apt update && sudo apt upgrade
```

```
username@username-virtualbox:~$ sudo apt install snapd
[sudo] password for username:
Reading package lists... Done
Building dependency tree     Done
Reading state information... Done
snapd is already the new version (2.51.1+20.04ubuntu2).
snapd set to manually installed.
Starting pkgProblemResolver with broken count: 0
Starting 2 pkgProblemResolver with broken count: 0
Done
The following packages were installed and are no longer
required:
  gstreamer1.0-nice gstreamer1.0-plugins-bad gstreamer1.0-
plugins-good gstreamer1.0-x libbs2b0
```

Now execute the given command to install the kphotoalbum package.

```
$ sudo apt-get install kphotoalbum
```

```
username@username-virtualbox:~$ sudo apt-get install
kphotoalbum
[sudo] password for username:
Reading package lists... Done
```

```
Building dependency tree
Reading state information... Done
Starting pkgProblemResolver with broken count: 0
Starting 2 pkgProblemResolver with broken count: 0
Done
The following packages were installed and are no longer
required:
  autoconf automake autotools-dev cpp-8 dvdauthor dvgrab
frei0r-plugins gcc gcc-8 gcc-8-base
```

The first screen of KPhotoAlbum is given below:

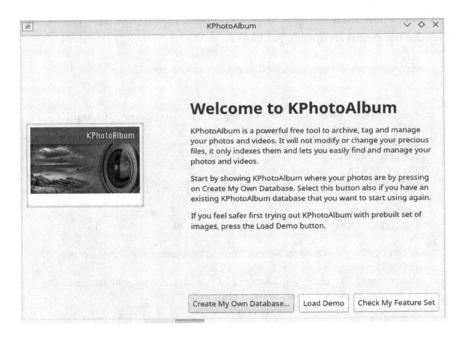

KPhotoAlbum Application window.

ARK APPLICATION

It is a file archiver and compressor developed by KDE and included in the KDE Applications software bundle. It supports various standard archive and compression formats, including zipping, 7z, rar, lha, and tar (uncompressed and compressed with, e.g., gzip, bzip2, lzip, or xz).

Features:

- It uses libarchive and karchive to support tar-based archives and a frontend for several command-line archivers.

- It can be integrated into Konqueror through KParts technology. After installing it, files can be added or extracted in/from the archives using Konqueror's context menus.

- Support for editing files in the archive with external programs. Files can also delete from the archive.

- Archive creation with drag and drop from the file manager.

The first screen of Ark is given below:

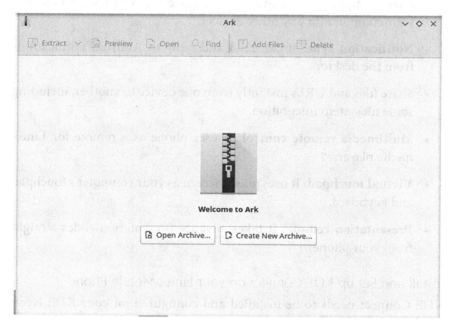

Ark Application window.

KDE CONNECT APPLICATION

It is a multi-platform application developed by KDE, facilitating wireless communications and data transfer between devices over local networks.

It is available in the repositories of other Linux Distributions with F-droid, Google Play Store for Android. Usually all distributions bundle

KDE Connect in their KDE Plasma desktop variant. KDE Connect has been reimplemented in GNOME desktop environment as GSConnect, which can be obtained from GNOME Extension Store.

Mechanism

KDE Connect utilizes various DBus interfaces from UI agnostic libraries for a specific operating system for its functioning.

Encryption

KDE Connect uses Transport Layer Security (TLS) encryption protocol for communication. It uses SFTP to mount devices and sends files.

Features:

- **Shared clipboard:** It can copy and paste between your phone and your computer (or any other device).

- **Notification sync:** It can read and reply to Android notifications from the desktop.

- Share files and URLs instantly from one device to another, including some filesystem integration.

- **Multimedia remote control:** It uses phone as a remote for Linux media players.

- **Virtual touchpad:** It uses phone screen as your computer's touchpad and keyboard.

- **Presentation remote:** It takes advance presentation slides straight from your phone.

Install and Set up KDE Connect on your Linux Mobile Phone

KDE Connect needs to be installed and configured on your KDE Neon involved.

1. On your KDE Neon system, go to Application and search for KDE Connect.

2. Install KDE Connect.

    We need to install KDE Connect and Indicator KDE Connect on our system. First, install KDE Connect. We currently use KDE Neon, so things might be slightly different when you run a further distribution.

3. Go to your software manager and search for KDE Connect or KDEConnect.

4. Click on KDEconnect and choose Install.
    If you would like to use the command line, use:

```
$ sudo apt Install kdeconnect
```

Now continue with installing Indicator KDE Connect.

5. Go to your software manager and search for Indicator KDE Connect or Indicator-KDEConnect.

6. Click on Indicator-KDEconnect and choose Install.
    If you would like to use the command line, type the following lines one by one followed by entering:

```
$ sudo add-apt-repository ppa:webupd8team/
indicator-kdeconnect
$ sudo apt update
$ sudo apt Install kdeconnect indicator-kdeconnect
```

How to Setup KDE Connect?
OK, now you have KDE Connect available on both your Android phone and your desktop.
    First, we will start the KDE Connect app on our phones.

7. So turn on your phone and start the newly installed KDE Connect app.

8. You now see an overview of all the devices with KDE Connect in your network.

9. You will be requested to request pairing. Click on Request Pairing.

10. You will get a pop-up to accept the request on your desktop, so do that.
    Suppose the pop-up disappears before having the chance to accept. Look in your panel/taskbar right and right-click on the KDE Connect indicator. Select the name of your Android device and select Pair.
    OK, so now you have finished the first part of pairing your Android device with your Linux desktop. Let's continue with the next part.

11. Go to your KDE Connect app on your Android device. Here you will be given with a dashboard with options like Send files, Multimedia control, etc. Here you also see a message that Plugins failed to load.

12. Tap on Notification sync and choose Open settings when asked to grant permission to access notifications.

13. Now check the option KDE Connect and choose for Allow.

    Now we have successfully paired our Android device with our desktop.

    It is possible to pair more than one Linux desktop with your Android device. In my case, I have two workstations and a notebook.

    You can follow the above steps to do the same setup for all your Linux devices.

    In an earlier step, you probably saw the message. Some plugins need permission to work. We need to do that first.

14. Go to your KDE Connections app on your phone and look for the message. Some plugins need permission to work.

15. Accept the request for permission for all these plugins.

    You probably see a message that some plugins have features disabled because of a lack of permission.

16. Accept the request for permission for this plugin.

The first screen of KDE Connect is given below:

KDE Connect Application window.

SPECTACLE APPLICATION

The spectacle is a simple application for capturing desktop screenshots. It captures images of the entire desktop, a single monitor, the currently active window, the window under the mouse, the rectangular region of the screen, etc. The images can print, sent to other applications for manipulation, or quickly saved.

Enable Snaps and Install a Spectacle

Snaps applications are packaged with dependencies to run on all popular Linux distributions from a single build. They update automatically and roll back gracefully.

Snaps are can installable from the Snap Store, an app store with an audience of millions.

Enable snapd in Terminal

Snap can install from the command line. Open the Konsole terminal window and enter the following:

```
$ sudo apt update
$ sudo apt install snapd
```

To install spectacle, use the following command:

```
$ sudo snap install spectacle
```

```
username@username-virtualbox:~$ sudo snap install spectacle
spectacle (candidate) 21.08.3 from KDE* installed
```

It is a multi-document, multi-view text editor by KDE. It features code folding, syntax highlighting, dynamic word wrap, an embedded console, an extensive plugin interface, and preliminary scripting support.

Installing Spectacle from Ubuntu Repositories

Installing spectacle from repositories is relatively straightforward and takes only a few minutes to complete.

Open a terminal using a keyboard shortcut, i.e., CTRL+ALT+T, and execute the below to update packages.

```
$ sudo apt update && sudo apt upgrade
```

```
username@username-virtualbox:~$ sudo apt install snapd
[sudo] password for username:
Reading package lists... Done
Building dependency tree     Done
Reading state information... Done
snapd is already the new version (2.51.1+20.04ubuntu2).
snapd set to manually installed.
Starting pkgProblemResolver with broken count: 0
Starting 2 pkgProblemResolver with broken count: 0
Done
The following packages were installed and are no longer
required:
  gstreamer1.0-nice gstreamer1.0-plugins-bad gstreamer1.0-
plugins-good gstreamer1.0-x libbs2b0
```

Features:

- It can capture Entire Desktop

- It can grab Current Monitor

- It can capture Active Window

- It can capture Rectangular Region

- It has keyboard shortcuts for taking screenshots

The first screen of Spectacle is given below:

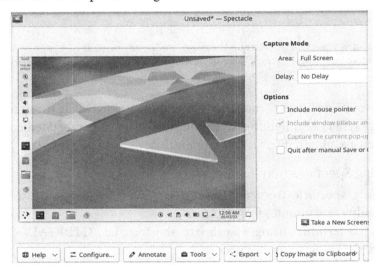

Spectacle Application window.

KCALC APPLICATION

- It has everything from a scientific calculator, plus.

- Trigonometric functions, logic operations, and statistical calculations.

- A results stack that enables convenient recall of previous calculation results.

- Precision is user-definable.

- It allows cut and paste of numbers.

- Its display colors and font are configurable, aiding usability.

- It can use of key-bindings make it easy to use without a pointing device.

Enable Snaps and Install a KCalc

Snaps applications are packaged with dependencies to run on all popular Linux distributions from a single build. They update automatically and roll back gracefully.

Snaps are can installable from the Snap Store, an app store with an audience of millions.

Enable snapd in Terminal

Snap can install from the command line. Open the Konsole terminal window and enter the following:

```
$ sudo apt update
$ sudo apt install snapd
```

To install kcalc, use the following command:

```
$ sudo snap install kcalc
```

```
username@username-virtualbox:~$ sudo snap install kcalc
[sudo] password for username:
kcalc 21.08.0 from KDE* installed
```

It is a multi-document, multi-view text editor by KDE. It features code folding, syntax highlighting, dynamic word wrap, an embedded console, an extensive plugin interface, and preliminary scripting support.

Installing KCalc from Ubuntu Repositories

Installing kcalc from repositories is relatively straightforward and takes only a few minutes to complete.

Open a terminal using a keyboard shortcut, i.e., CTRL+ALT+T, and execute the below to update packages.

```
$ sudo apt update && sudo apt upgrade
```

```
username@username-virtualbox:~$ sudo apt install snapd
[sudo] password for username:
Reading package lists... Done
Building dependency tree      Done
Reading state information... Done
snapd is already the new version (2.51.1+20.04ubuntu2).
snapd set to manually installed.
Starting pkgProblemResolver with broken count: 0
Starting 2 pkgProblemResolver with broken count: 0
Done
The following packages were installed and are no longer
required:
   gstreamer1.0-nice gstreamer1.0-plugins-bad gstreamer1.0-
plugins-good gstreamer1.0-x libbs2b0
```

The first screen of Kcalc is given below:

Kcalc Application window.

KWALLETMANAGER APPLICATION

It is a tool to manage the passwords on your system. Using the Frameworks wallet subsystem allows you to keep secret access and manage every application's passwords that link with the wallet.

Install kwallet-pam for the PAM compatible module to unlock KDE Wallet on login. The current KWallet password must be the same as the current user password.

Installing KWalletManager from Ubuntu Repositories

Installing KWalletManager from repositories is relatively straightforward and takes only a few minutes to complete.

Open a terminal using a keyboard shortcut, i.e., CTRL+ALT+T, and execute the below to update packages.

```
$ sudo apt update && sudo apt upgrade
```

```
username@username-virtualbox:~$ sudo apt install snapd
[sudo] password for username:
Reading package lists... Done
Building dependency tree     Done
Reading state information... Done
snapd is already the new version (2.51.1+20.04ubuntu2).
snapd set to manually installed.
Starting pkgProblemResolver with broken count: 0
Starting 2 pkgProblemResolver with broken count: 0
Done
The following packages were installed and are no longer
required:
  gstreamer1.0-nice gstreamer1.0-plugins-bad gstreamer1.0-
plugins-good gstreamer1.0-x libbs2b0
```

To install kwalletmanager, use the following command:

```
$ sudo apt-get install kwalletmanager
```

```
username@username-virtualbox:~$ sudo apt-get install
kwalletmanager
[sudo] password for username:
Reading package lists... Done
Building dependency tree
```

```
Reading state information... Done
kwalletmanager is already the newest version
(4:21.12.1-0xneon+20.04+focal+release+build28).
kwalletmanager set to manually installed.
Starting pkgProblemResolver with broken count: 0
Starting 2 pkgProblemResolver with broken count: 0
Done
The following packages were installed and are no longer
required:
  autoconf automake autotools-dev cpp-8 dvdauthor dvgrab
frei0r-plugins gcc gcc-8 gcc-8-base
  gcc-9 gdal-data gfortran gfortran-8 gfortran-9
gstreamer1.0-nice gstreamer1.0-plugins-bad
```

Features:

- Wallets can drag from the KWalletManager window. It allows dragging the wallet to a file browser window, where you can easily choose to copy, move, and link the wallet.

- You can use this to save a wallet to portable media, such as a USB keychain, so you can take passwords with you to work or on vacation and still have easy access to important sites.

PLASMA-DISCOVER

It is an all-in-one software manager and "app store" built around KDE Plasma which works in any desktop environment. It is user-friendly also has an attractive look. It supports multiple package management systems and snaps and flatpak, which is the default software manager on other Linux distributions.

It helps to find and install applications, games, and tools. You can also search or browse by their category, look at screenshots and read reviews to pick the perfect app.

With Discover, you can manage software from multiple sources, including your operating system's software repository, Flatpak repos, the Snap store, or even AppImages from store.kde.org.

It shows a list of categories to the left, software in the middle, and a detailed description of that software to the right after clicking on a piece of software.

Discoverer's root categories are Applications where all software are located. Then there are Application addons with addons specific to KDE software and Plasma addons with addons specific to KDE's Plasma desktop environment. The Application is helpful for those not using the KDE's Plasma desktop environment. It also allows you to find, install, and manage addons for Plasma and all your favorite KDE apps.

Installing Plasma-Discover from Ubuntu Repositories

Installing plasma-discover from repositories is relatively straightforward and takes only a few minutes to complete.

Open a terminal using a keyboard shortcut, i.e., CTRL+ALT+T, and execute the below to update packages.

```
$ sudo apt update && sudo apt upgrade
```

```
username@username-virtualbox:~$ sudo apt install snapd
[sudo] password for username:
Reading package lists... Done
Building dependency tree      Done
Reading state information... Done
snapd is already the new version (2.51.1+20.04ubuntu2).
snapd set to manually installed.
Starting pkgProblemResolver with broken count: 0
Starting 2 pkgProblemResolver with broken count: 0
Done
The following packages were installed and are no longer
required:
   gstreamer1.0-nice gstreamer1.0-plugins-bad gstreamer1.0-
plugins-good gstreamer1.0-x libbs2b0
```

To install plasma-discover, use the following command:

```
$ sudo apt-get install plasma-discover
```

```
sername@username-virtualbox:~$ sudo apt-get install
plasma-discover
Reading package lists... Done
Building dependency tree
Reading state information... Done
plasma-discover is already the newest version (5.23.5-0xneo
n+20.04+focal+release+build49).
plasma-discover set to manually installed.
Starting pkgProblemResolver with broken count: 0
```

```
Starting 2 pkgProblemResolver with broken count: 0
Done
The following packages were installed and are no longer
required:
  autoconf automake autotools-dev cpp-8 dvdauthor dvgrab
frei0r-plugins gcc gcc-8 gcc-8-base
```

The first screen of plasma-discover is given below:

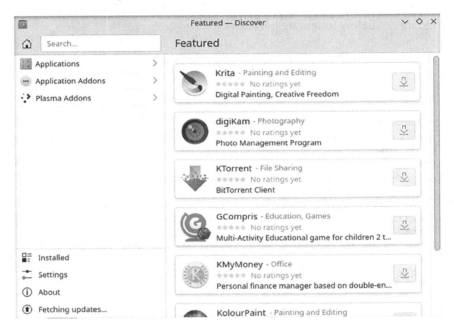

Plasma Discover Application window.

KOLOURPAINT APPLICATION

It is a free, open source graphics editor by KDE. It is similar to Microsoft Paint but has additional features such as transparency, color balance, and image rotation.

Installing KolourPaint from Ubuntu Repositories

Installing kolourpaint from repositories is relatively straightforward and takes only a few minutes to complete.

Open a terminal using a keyboard shortcut, i.e., CTRL+ALT+T, and execute the below to update packages.

```
$ sudo apt update && sudo apt upgrade
```

```
username@username-virtualbox:~$ sudo apt install snapd
[sudo] password for username:
Reading package lists... Done
Building dependency tree      Done
Reading state information... Done
snapd is already the new version (2.51.1+20.04ubuntu2).
snapd set to manually installed.
Starting pkgProblemResolver with broken count: 0
Starting 2 pkgProblemResolver with broken count: 0
Done
The following packages were installed and are no longer
required:
  gstreamer1.0-nice gstreamer1.0-plugins-bad gstreamer1.0-
plugins-good gstreamer1.0-x libbs2b0
```

To install plasma-discover, use the following command:

```
$ sudo apt-get install kolourpaint
```

```
username@username-virtualbox:~$ sudo apt-get install
kolourpaint
[sudo] password for username:
Reading package lists... Done
Building dependency tree
Reading state information... Done
Starting pkgProblemResolver with broken count: 0
Starting 2 pkgProblemResolver with broken count: 0
Done
The following packages were installed and are no longer
required:
  autoconf automake autotools-dev cpp-8 dvdauthor dvgrab
frei0r-plugins gcc gcc-8 gcc-8-base
  gcc-9 gdal-data gfortran gfortran-8 gfortran-9
gstreamer1.0-nice gstreamer1.0-plugins-bad
```

Its aims are too simple to understand, providing functionality targeted toward the average user. KolourPaint is designed for everyday work such as:

- **Painting:** drawing diagrams and "finger painting."
- Image Manipulation used for editing screenshots and photos; applying effects.

- Icon Editing represents the drawing clipart and logos with transparency.

- In Version K, Desktop Environment 3.3 replaced KPaint as the standard simple painting application.

KolourPaint has a port to Microsoft Windows [citation needed] as part of the KDE on Windows initiative. KolourPaint also has ports to MacOS.gcc-9 gdal-data gfortran gfortran-8 gfortran-9 gstreamer1.0-nice gstreamer1.0-plugins-bad.

Features:

- It supports drawing various shapes such as lines, rectangles, rounded rectangles, ovals, polygons, curves, lines, and text.

- Has color picker and selections.

- Rotation, monochrome, and other advanced effects.

The first screen of kolourpaint is given below:

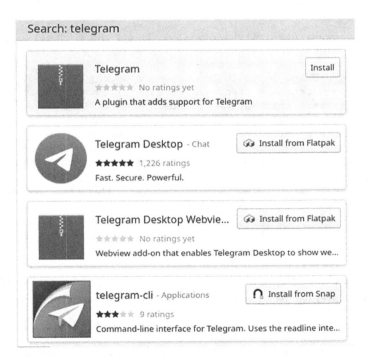

kolourpaint Application window.

ELISA APPLICATION

Elisa is a music player created by the KDE community. It is simple and nice to use.

While the evident "focus" for the player is on integration with the KDE Plasma desktop, it has ambitions beyond it. Elisa is a first-class option for users of Linux desktop environments, like GNOME Shell and users of Windows and Android. Its first formal release of this app is not packed full of extra bells and whistles yet, but the core music player functionality is present and working.

Installing Elisa from Ubuntu Repositories

Installing elisa from repositories is relatively straightforward and takes only a few minutes to complete.

Open a terminal using a keyboard shortcut, i.e., CTRL+ALT+T, and execute the below to update packages.

```
$ sudo apt update && sudo apt upgrade
```

```
username@username-virtualbox:~$ sudo apt install snapd
[sudo] password for username:
Reading package lists... Done
Building dependency tree      Done
Reading state information... Done
snapd is already the new version (2.51.1+20.04ubuntu2).
snapd set to manually installed.
Starting pkgProblemResolver with broken count: 0
Starting 2 pkgProblemResolver with broken count: 0
Done
The following packages were  installed and are no longer
required:
  gstreamer1.0-nice gstreamer1.0-plugins-bad gstreamer1.0-
plugins-good gstreamer1.0-x libbs2b0
```

To install plasma-discover, use the following command:

```
$ sudo apt-get install elisa
```

```
username@username-virtualbox:~$ sudo apt-get install elisa
Reading package lists... Done
Building dependency tree
Reading state information... Done
```

```
Starting pkgProblemResolver with broken count: 0
Starting 2 pkgProblemResolver with broken count: 0
Done
The following packages were installed and are no longer
required:
  autoconf automake autotools-dev cpp-8 dvdauthor dvgrab
frei0r-plugins gcc gcc-8 gcc-8-base
  gcc-9 gdal-data gfortran gfortran-8 gfortran-9
gstreamer1.0-nice gstreamer1.0-plugins-bad
  gstreamer1.0-plugins-good gstreamer1.0-x ibverbs-
providers kdenlive-data libarmadillo9
```

Features:

- Anyone can browse music by album, artist, or tracks

- Supports working search

- You can create and manage playlists and view track metadata

- Baloo indexing support

- Supports for HiDPI displays

The first screen of Elisa is given below:

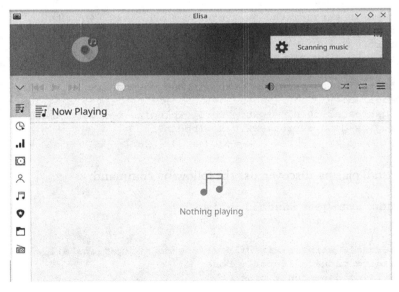

Elisa Application window.

CHAPTER SUMMARY

We have discussed the KDE application, its working and installation using the command line in your system with user interface guide of each. We also have covered its features and use of every desktop environment.

CHAPTER 4

Doing More with KDE

IN THIS CHAPTER

➢ Doing more with KDE

➢ Introduction of Qt

➢ History of Qt

➢ List of language bindings for Qt

➢ Desktop environments based on GTK

➢ KDE frameworks

Chapter 3 is all about the application based on KDE. We can install/remove all these applications using the command line and Software application.

Now we will discuss Qt that was initially developed by Trolltech. Nokia acquired the company in 2008. In August 2012, Digia acquired Qt software technologies from Nokia in the Finnish development company. A Qt Project was created so that the development of open source Qt continues. The website for the open source Qt toolkit can be found at qt.io. Qt is being developed by the Qt Company, a subsidiary of Digia, and the project is under open source control, involving individual developers and firms.

WHAT IS Qt?

It is a cross-platform development framework for desktop, mobile, and embedded. It can support various platforms, including Linux, OS X, Windows, VxWorks, QNX, Android, iOS, BlackBerry, Sailfish OS, etc.

DOI: 10.1201/9781003309406-4

It is not a programming language on its own. It is a framework written in C++. The Meta-Object Compiler (MOC) is a preprocessor used to extend the C++ language with features like signals and slots. Before any compilation step, the MOC parses the source files written in Qt-extended C++ and generates standard-compliant C++ sources from them. Thus, the framework and applications/libraries can be compiled by any standard-compliant C++ compiler like Clang, GCC, ICC, MinGW, and MSVC.

THE Qt COMPANY AND THE Qt PROJECT

The development of Qt was started in 1990 by the Norwegian programmers Eirik Chambe-Eng and Haavard Nord. Trolltech, which sold Qt licenses, also provided support. It went through several acquisitions over the years. Today Trolltech is named The Qt Company and a wholly-owned subsidiary of Digia Plc in Finland. The Qt Company is the core driver behind Qt, and a more extensive alliance currently developing it: The Qt Project consists of many companies and individuals around the globe and follows a meritocratic governance model.

Everyone who wants individuals and companies can join the effort. Many methods can contribute to the Qt Project by writing code or documentation for the framework, helping other users on the forum, reporting bugs.

Qt is available under various licenses. The company sells commercial licenses, but Qt is also known as free software under several GPL and the LGPL (Licensing FAQ).

Although any build system can use with Qt, Qt brings its make. It is a cross-platform frontend for platform-native build systems, like GNU Make, Visual Studio, and Xcode.

CMake is a popular alternative to build Qt projects. Qt 4 support was integrated years ago, and Qt 5 provided support early.

Recently, a new player entered the game: The Qt Build Suite, a.k.a Qbs. Qbs is a QML-based build system that also provides support for Javascript. This build system not only includes building capability but also packaging like CMake.

Now we are going to discuss the following terms in the above lines given below.

qmake

It is a tool that can automate the generation of Makefiles for projects, i.e., acts as a build system tool. This section of the official Qt documentation is dedicated to this particular tool. The idea behind this page is to collect some material tips and tricks that can be useful.

The qmake tool simplifies the build process for development projects across various platforms. It can automate the generation of Makefiles so that only a few pieces of information are required to create each Makefile. You can use it for any software project, whether written with Qt or not. It generates a Makefile based on the information in a project file. The developer creates simple project files, but more sophisticated ones can make for complex projects.

It contains extra features to support development with Qt that automatically builds rules for MOC and UIC. It can generate projects for Microsoft Visual studio without requiring the developer to change the project file.

Overview

It provides a project-oriented system for managing the process for libraries, applications, and other components. It gives control over the source files and allows each of the steps in the process to be described mannerly within a single file. qmake.

What Is a Project?

Projects are described by the project (.pro) files. qmake tool uses the information within the files to generate Makefiles containing all the commands needed to build each project. Project files typically have a list of source and header files, general configuration information, and application-specific details, like a list of extra libraries to link against or a list of additional include paths to use.

Project files can contain several elements, including comments, variable declarations, built-in functions, and control structures. It is necessary to declare the source and header files used to build the project with basic configuration options in most simple projects.

It would be best to run qmake in your project's top-level directory for basic tasks to generate a Makefile. You can then run your platform's make a tool to build the project.

For more information about the variables that qmake uses when configuring the build process.

Using Third-Party Libraries

The Third-Party Libraries shows you how to use simple Third-Party Libraries in your Qt project.

GNU Make

It is a tool that controls the generation of executables and other non-source files of a program from the program's source files.

Make knows how to build a program from a file called the Makefile, which lists each of the non-source files and computes it from other files. When you write any program, you should write a Makefile to make it possible to use Make to build and install the program.

In software development, Make is a build automation tool that automatically builds programs and libraries from source code by reading Makefiles, which specify how to derive the target program. Though integrated development environments features can also be used to manage a build process, Make remains widely used, especially in Unix and Unix-like operating systems.

Besides building programs, Make can manage any project where some files must be updated automatically whenever others change.

MakeFile

Make can search the current directory for the Makefile, e.g., GNU Make searches files for a file named one of GNUmakefile, Makefile then runs the specified target from that file.

The Makefile language resembles declarative programming. One problem in build automation is tailoring a build process to a given platform. For example, the compiler used on one platform might not accept the same options as the one used on another. Make does not sufficiently handle it. This problem is typically addressed by generating platform-specific build instructions, which Make processes. Standard tools for this process are Autoconf, CMake, or GYP.

Makefiles may contain five kinds of things:

- An explicit rule says when and how to remake more files, called the rule's targets. It lists the other files that targets depend on, called the target's prerequisites, and gives a method to create or update the targets.

- An implicit rule says when and how to remake a class of files based on their names. It describes how a target depends on a file with a similar name and gives a method to create or update such a target.

- A variable definition specifies a text string value for a variable that can substitute into the text later.

- A directive is an instruction for making something special while reading the Makefile, such as reading another.

- Lines starting with # are used for comments.

Capabilities of Make

- It can enable the end-user to build and install your package without knowing how that is done.

- Its figure-out files need to update based on which origin files have changed. It also determines the proper order for updating files if one non-source file depends on another non-source file.

- If you change a source file and then Make, it does not need to recompile all of your programs. It updates those non-source files that depend directly or indirectly on the changed source files.

- It is not limited to any particular language. For each non-source file, the Makefile specifies the shell commands to run it. These shell commands can run a compiler to produce an object file. The linker to create an executable, update a library, or TeX or Makeinfo to format documentation.

- It is not limited to building a package. You can use it to control installing or deinstalling a package, generate tags tables, or anything else you want to do make it worthwhile writing down how to do it.

Make Rules and Targets

A rule in the Makefile tells Makes to execute a series of commands to build a target file from source files. It specifies a list of dependencies of the target file. This list should include all files used as inputs to the commands in the rule.

Here is a simple rule looks like:

```
target:    dependencies.
commands
..
```

When you run, Make it specify particular targets to update; otherwise, Make updates to the first target listed in the Makefile. Any target files needed as input for generating these targets must be updated first.

Make uses the Makefile to determine which target files should be brought up-to-date and then decide which needs to be updated. If a file is newer than all of its dependencies, it is already up-to-date. It does not need to regenerate. The other target files also need to be updated in the proper order.

Advantages of GNU Make

GNU Make has many powerful features in Makefiles beyond what other Make versions have. It can regenerate, use, then delete intermediate files which need not save.

It has a few simple features that are very convenient. For example, the -o file option says "pretend that source file has not changed, even though it has changed." It is beneficial to add a new macro to a header file. Most versions of Make are recompiled all the source files that use the header file. It gives a way to avoid recompilation where you know to change to the header file does not require it. However, the critical contrast between GNU Make and most Make versions is that GNU Make is free software.

Microsoft Visual Studio

It is an IDE from Microsoft. It develops computer programs and websites, web apps, services, and mobile apps. It uses software development platforms such as API, Forms, Presentation Foundation, Store, and Silverlight. It can produce both native and managed code.

It also includes a code editor supporting IntelliSense and code refactoring. The debugger works both as a source-level debugger and a machine-level debugger. Other built-in tools are a code profiler, designer for building graphical user interface (GUI) applications, web designer, class designer, and database schema designer. It accepts plug-ins that can expand the functionality at every level, including adding support for source control systems and are new toolsets like editors and visual designers.

It supports 36 programming languages and a debugger to support nearly any programming language, provided a language-specific service exists. Built-in languages include C, C++, Visual Basic .NET, C#, F#, JavaScript, TypeScript, XML, XSLT, HTML, and CSS. It also supports other languages, such as Python, Ruby, Node.js, and M, are available via plug-ins. Java was supported in the past.

The most basic edition is the Community edition which is available free. The slogan for the Community edition is "Free, fully-featured IDE for beginners, open source and particular developers."

The current production-ready version is 2022, with older versions 2013 2015 on Extended Support, 2017, and 2019 on Mainstream Support.

Features

- **Code editor:** A code editor supports syntax highlighting code completion using IntelliSense for variables, methods, loops, functions, and LINQ queries. IntelliSense is kept for the included languages and XML, Cascading Style Sheets, and JavaScript when developing websites and web applications. It has autocompleted suggestions appear in a modeless list box over the code editor window, in the proximity of the editing cursor. Visual Studio 2008 onward can be made temporarily semitransparent to see the code obstructed by it. It is used for all supported languages.

- **Debugger:** It has a debugger that works both as a source-level debugger and a machine-level debugger. It works with managed code and native code that can use for debugging applications written in any language supported by Visual Studio. It can attach to running processes, monitor, and debug those processes. If the source code for the running process is available, it displays the code as it runs. If the code is not available, it can show the disassembly. The Visual Studio debugger can create memory dumps and load them later for debugging. Multi-threaded programs are supported.

- **Designer:** Visual Studio includes a host of graphic designers to aid in developing applications. These tools include:

  - **Windows Forms Designer:** It is used to build GUI applications using Windows Forms. The layout can control by housing the controls inside other containers or locking them to the side of the form. Controls that display data like textbox, list box, and grid view can be bound to data sources like databases or queries.

  - **WPF Designer:** It is codenamed. Cider was introduced with Visual Studio 2008. It supports the drag and drops metaphor and author user interfaces targeting Windows Presentation Foundation (WPF). It supports all WPF functionality, including data binding and automatic layout management. It generates XAML code for the UI.

- **Extensibility:** It allows developers to write extensions for Visual Studio to extend its capabilities. These extensions "plug into" Visual Studio and extend its functionality. It comes in the form of macros, add-ins, and packages. Macros can represent repeatable tasks and actions that developers can record programmatically for saving, replaying, and distributing. Macros cannot implement new commands or create tool windows. They are written using Visual Basic and are not compiled.

What is Xcode?

It is an integrated development environment (IDE) created by Apple company for developing software for their operating system macOS, iOS, watchOS, and tvOS. It is the officially supported tool for creating and publishing apps to the App Store, which is designed for beginners and experienced developers.

It includes all of the tools needed to create an app within one software package:

- A text editor

- A compiler

- A build system

With Xcode, you can quickly write, compile, and debug any application, and when you have finished, you can submit your application to the App store. It contains several tools to help the development process move quickly so that seasoned developers can create apps lightning fast, and beginners face less confusion and barriers to creating a great application.

As a code editor, Xcode supports a vast variety of programming languages – C, C++, Objective-C, Objective-C++, Java, AppleScript, Python, Ruby, ResEdit, and Swift. It uses Cocoa, Carbon, and Java programming models.

Xcode is designed to give you one window in which to work as a developer. It has a source code checker and autocompletes feature, making writing source code much more straightforward. When you build a project, you can select from the available templates to give you a basic framework to expand. These features are helpful to new developers as they give you a crutch to lean on as you learn. Advanced developers will find these features useful to streamline their workflow and faster application development.

Xcode is the support to development apps by Apple. So if you are interested in building iOS or macOS apps, you can use it. There are third-party solutions that do not require to use of Xcode. However, these are not supported by Apple, and there are usually issues with these solutions.

Xcode comes with great debugging tools that allow developers to solve problems in their apps faster. It also comes with project management tools that will enable you to manage your image assets and code files in an organized way.

CMake

It is an open source, cross-platform family of tools designed to build, test, and package software, package, and install software using a compiler-independent method. It can control the software compilation process utilizing the simple platform and compiler-independent configuration files and generates native Makefiles and workspaces in the compiler environment of your choice. Kitware created the suite of CMake tools in response to the need for a robust, cross-platform environment for open source projects like ITK and VTK.

Notable applications using CMake:

- Netflix

- Inria

- KDE

- ReactOS

- The HDF Group

- Second Life

It is cross-platform free and open source software for building automation testing in software development, and it is not a build system. Instead, it generates another system build files. It can support directory hierarchies and applications that depend on numerous libraries. It is used with native build environments such as Make, Qt Creator, Ninja, Android Studio, Apple's Xcode, and Microsoft Visual Studio. It has minimal dependencies, requiring only a C++ compiler on its build system. CMake is distributed as open source software under a permissive New BSD license.

Features

A key feature is placing compiler outputs outside the source tree. It enables multiple builds from the same source tree and cross-compilation. It keeps the source tree separate, ensuring that removing a build directory will not remove the source files. The users are not protected from removing the source code folder.

Flexible Project Structure

It can locate system-wide and user-specified files and libraries. Its locations are stored in a cache, tailored before generating the target build files. The cache can edit with a graphical editor, which is shipped with CMake.

CMake well supports complicated directory hierarchies and applications that rely on several libraries. For instance, CMake can accommodate a project with multiple toolkits or libraries with various directories. In addition, it can work with projects that require executables to be created before generating code. Its open source, extensible design allows CMake to be adapted as necessary for specific projects.

IDEs Configuration Support

It can generate project files for several popular IDEs, such as Microsoft Visual Studio, Xcode, and Eclipse CDT. It can produce build scripts for MSBuild, Ninja, NMake on Microsoft Windows, Ninja, Unix Make on Unix platforms such as Linux, macOS, Cygwin.

Compiler Feature Detection

CMake allows the specification of features that the compiler must support to compile the target program or library.

Compilers

It supports an extensive list of compilers, including Apple Clang, Clang, GNU GCC, MSVC, Oracle Developer Studio, and Intel C++ Compile.

Qbs

It is a build automation tool designed to manage the build process of software projects across multiple platforms.

Features

Qbs provides the following benefits such as:

- **It supports the declarative paradigm:** With declarative language, Qbs enables you to express intent rather than specifying single build steps. It provides the appropriate level of abstraction for a build system. For example, dependencies can create between products. The target artifacts of the dependence can be used as input to the build rules in the context of the depending development. In addition, you can export dependencies and properties to other products.

  Qbs is modular with clean interfaces between modules. A module is a collection of language items used for building a product if the product depends on the module. The properties set for a module are used to control the behavior of the toolchain used to do the module.

- **Also well-defined language:** It is specified in a QML dialect and concise, easy-to-learn, and intuitive language used successfully in the Qt project. Its core is declarative, but it can extend with JavaScript snippets for extra flexibility.

  It can build applications based on the information in a project file. Each project file specifies one project that can contain several products. You set the type of the product, such as an application, and the dependencies the product has on other products.

  The product type determines the rules that Qbs applies to produce artifacts from input files. For example, the input files can be divided according to their style or purpose. A group can also use to attach properties to products.

- **It has a platform and programming language independence:** Qbs can be used for the software project, programming language, toolkit, or libraries and has built-in support for building applications for Windows, Android, Linux, macOS, iOS, watchOS, QNX, etc. FreeBSD and cross-compilation. It can extend to support other platforms.

- **It can correct and fast incremental builds:** Qbs automatically use multiprocessor and multicore systems to achieve maximum build parallelization. By default, running qbs without any arguments is equivalent to making -j<n> where n is the number of CPU cores.

Also, it allows the number of concurrent jobs to be explicitly specified using its own -j option.

Qbs knows the whole project and therefore builds remain correct even when you make sub-projects because Qbs ensures that all dependencies are built. It virtually eliminates the need for clean builds.

- It has an extensible architecture

- It has easy integration to IDEs

VISUAL STUDIO CODE

It provides the qbs-community plugin that gives accurate information about the build progress and displays a project tree that can reflect the project's logical structure. Also, it can provide low-level details, such as the file system structure.

Qt QUICK

It is a high-level technology that allows developers and UI designers to work together to create various animated, touch-enabled UIs, and lightweight applications. It includes also go tons of work.

It includes a visual editor that allows UI designers to cooperate, working on the same code in a looping approach.

QML stands for Qt Meta-Object Language. It is an easy to use, declarative language.

QtDeclarative is a new module in the Qt library that enables a new declarative programming approach.

C++ programming skills are needed to use Qt Quick. The bindings are based on Qt and can be extended from C++ and other languages, limited only by your creativity.

Scope (Qt Creator and Quick):

- QML project wizard and project management (new file format for pure QML applications)

- Advanced QML editor with syntax highlighting, code completion, integrated help features, and more

- **Qt Quick Designer:** Visual WYSIWYG editor to create Qt Quick user interfaces (technical preview)

- **Qt Quick Components:** Common UI Elements that fit into platform Look and Feel

QML vs. Widget-Based GUI

Qt beginners often ask: What option will be the best for creating my user interface. With Qt, there are three techniques (which can be integrated):

- using Qt Designer to create *.ui files

- an XML-based UI description coding the setup of your UI in C++ with Qt widgets classes

- write or visually design ML files

IDE (Integrated Development Environment)

Qt comes with its Integrated Development Environment named Qt Creator. It can run on Linux, OS X, and Windows. It offers intelligent code completion, syntax highlighting, an integrated help system, debugger, profiler integration, and all major version control systems, for example, git, Bazaar. Moreover, Qt Creator developers on Windows can use Qt's Visual Studio Add-in. Other IDEs like KDevelop on KDE can also use.

Qt has features to support internationalization (i18n) and localization (l10n). The tool Qt Linguist and its companion's update, release, and convert make it easy to translate applications to locale languages. Qt supports most languages and writing systems that are in use today.

Qt Quick

It is a free software application framework developed and maintained by the Qt Project within the Qt framework. It provides a way of building custom, dynamic GUIs with fluid transitions and effects, becoming more common, especially in mobile devices. It includes a scripting language called QML.

Qt Declarative is a runtime interpreter that can read the Qt declarative user interface definition and QML data and display its described UI. The QML syntax allows JavaScript to provide the logic.

Qt is a GUI toolkit that provides modules for cross-platform development in networking, databases, OpenGL, web technologies, sensors, communications protocols such as Bluetooth, serial ports, NFC), XML, and JSON processing, printing, PDF generation, and much more.

Widgets

Using Qt, your GUIs can be written directly in C++ using its Widgets module. Qt also comes with an interactive tool called Qt Designer, which functions as a code generator for Widgets-based GUIs. Qt Designer can use stand-alone but is also integrated into Qt Creator.

We will learn basic Qt knowledge by implementing a simple application using C++ and the Qt Widgets module. The application is a text editor which allows you to create a text file, and you can save it, print it, reopen, and edit it again. You can also set the font to be used.

The Qt Widgets module can provide a set of UI elements to create classic desktop user interfaces.

Use the following directive to include the definitions of the module's classes:

```
#include <QtWidgets>
```

Add a line to the qmake .pro file to link against the module:

```
QT += widgets
```

These are the primary elements for creating user interfaces in Qt. It can also display data and status information, receive user input, and provide a container for other widgets that should be grouped. These widgets are not embedded in a parent widget is called a window.

The QWidget class provides the essential capability to render and handle user input events to the screen. All user interface elements that Qt provides are either subclasses or are used in connection with a QWidget subclass. Creating custom widgets is done by subclassing QWidget or a suitable subclass and reimplementing the virtual event handlers.

Handlers are given below:

- Window and Dialog Widgets

- Application Main Window

- Dialog Windows

- Keyboard Focus in Widgets

QWidget Class

The widget is part of the user interface. It works with the mouse, keyboard, and any other events from the window system and paints a representation of itself on the screen. Every widget is rectangular. They are sorted in a Z-order and clipped by their parent and the widgets in front of it.

A window is not embedded in a parent widget. Windows have a frame and a title bar, and it is also possible to create windows without such decoration using suitable window flags. In Qt programming, QMainWindow and the other subclasses of QDialog are the common window types. Each widget's constructor accepts only two standard arguments given below:

```
QWidget *parent = nullptr
```

It is the parent of the new widget. The new widget will have a window if it is (the default) nullptr. If it is then, it will be a child of the parent and be constrained by its geometry.

```
Qt::WindowFlags f = { } (where available)
```

By default, it sets the window flags is suitable for almost all widgets, but to get, for example, a window without a window system frame, you must use special flags.

It has many member functions, but some of them have direct functionality. For example, it has a font property. Many subclasses provide actual functionality, such as QLabel, QPushButton, QListWidget, and QTabWidget.

Class	Purpose
QWidgetScrollListWidget	A wrapper around QWidgetListWidget to provide scrolling.
QWidgetListWidget	The widget that contains the items.
QWidgetListItem	The items that can be put in the list. Can contain any number of sub-widgets, of any type.
QWidgetListMimeData	The MIME data is used to support drag-and-drop between multiple QWidgetListWidget.

QLabel

It is used for displaying text or an image. No user interaction functionality is provided. The label's visual appearance can be configured in various ways, and it can use for specifying a focus key for another widget.

A QLabel can also contain any of the following content types:

Content	Setting
Plain text	It passes a QString to setText().
Rich text	It passes a QString that contains rich text to setText().
A pixmap	It passes a QPixmap to setPixmap().
A movie	It passesa QMovie to setMovie().
A number	It passes an int or a double to setNum(), which converts the number to plain text.
Nothing	The same as an empty plain text. It is the default. Set by clear().

It is often used as a label for an interactive widget. It provides a useful mechanism for adding a mnemonic will set the keyboard focus to the other widget called the QLabel's "buddy." For example:

```
QLineEdit *phoneEdit = new QLineEdit(this);
QLabel *phoneLabel = new QLabel("&Phone:", this);
phoneLabel->setBuddy(phoneEdit);
```

In this example, keyboard focus is transferred to the label's buddy, the QLineEdit, when the user presses Alt+P. If the buddy were a button (inheriting from QAbstractButton), triggering the mnemonic would emulate a button click.

QPushbutton

The push-button, or command button, is perhaps the most commonly used widget in any GUI. Click a button to command to perform some action or answer a question. Standard buttons are OK, Apply, Cancel, Close, Yes, No, and Help.

A command button is rectangular and displays a text label describing its action. A shortcut key can specify by preceding the preferred character with an ampersand. For example:

```
QPushButton *button = new QPushButton("&Download",
this);
```

Push buttons can display a textual label and a small icon. These can be set by using the constructors and changed using setText() and setIcon(). When the button is disabled, the appearance of the text and icon will manipulate concerning the GUI style to make the button look "disabled."

A push-button emits the signal clicked() when activated by the mouse, the Spacebar, or a keyboard shortcut. Push buttons provide less commonly used signals. For example, pressed() signal and released() signal.

Command buttons are by default auto-default buttons, and they become the default push-button get when they receive the keyboard input focus. A push-button is activated when the user presses the Enter in a dialog. You can change it with setAutoDefault(). Auto-default buttons reserve a little extra space to draw a default-button indicator. If you don't want extra space around buttons, call setAutoDefault(false).

As a general rule, use a push-button when the application or dialog window performs when the user clicks on it like Apply, Cancel, Close, and Help). The widget should have a comprehensive, rectangular shape with a text label. Small, typically square buttons that change the window's state rather than acting, such as the buttons in the top-right corner of the QFileDialog, do not command buttons but tool buttons. Qt provides a particular class (QToolButton) for these buttons.

QListWidget

It is a class that provides a list view similar to QListView, but with a classic item-based interface for adding and removing items. It uses an internal model to manage each QListWidgetItem in the list.

Use the QListView class with a standard model for a more flexible list view widget.

List widgets are constructed in the way as other widgets:

```
QListWidget *listWidget = new QListWidget(this);
```

The selectionMode() of a list widget determines items in the list that can be selected simultaneously, and complex selections of items can create. It can be set with the set selection mode() function.

There are two ways to add items to the list:

- Constructed with the list widget as their parent widget.

- Constructed with no parent widget and added to the list later.

If a list widget already exists when the items are constructed, the first method is easier to use:

```
new QListWidgetItem(tr("Oak"), listWidget);
new QListWidgetItem(tr("Fir"), listWidget);
new QListWidgetItem(tr("Pine"), listWidget);
```

It should be constructed without a parent widget to add a new item into the list at a specific position. The insertItem() function should then place within the list. The list widget will take ownership of all the items.

```
QListWidgetItem *new_Item = new QListWidgetItem;
newItem-> setText(item_Text);
listWidget->insertItem(row, new_Item);
```

For multiple items, useinsertItems(). The number of items is found with the count() function. To remove items from the list, you can use takeItem().

The current item can find with currentItem() and change with setCurrentItem(). The user can change the contemporary item by navigating with the keyboard or clicking on a different item. When the current item changes, the currentItemChanged() signal is emitted with the new current item and the previously current item.

QTabWidget

A tab widget provides a tab bar and a "page area" used to display pages related to each tab. The tab bar is displayed over the page area by default, but different configurations are available. Each tab is linked with a different widget called a page. Only the active page is shown in the page area, rest all the other pages are hidden. The user can offer a separate page by clicking on its tab or by pressing its Alt+letter shortcut if it has one.

The usual way to use QTabWidget is to do the following:

- Create a QTabWidget.

- Create a QWidget for individual pages in the tab dialog, but do not specify parent widgets for them.

- Insert child widgets into the page widget, using layouts to position them as usual.

- Call addTab() or insertTab() to put the page widgets into the tab widget, giving each tab a suitable label with an optional keyboard shortcut.

The position of the tabs is known by tabPosition and their shape by tabShape.

The signal currentChanged() is executed when the user selects a page. The current page index is available by currentIndex(), the current page widget using currentWidget(). You can receive a pointer to a page widget with a given index by the widget(). You can find the index position of a widget with indexOf(). You can use setCurrentWidget()/setCurrentIndex() to show a specific page.

You can also change a tab's text and icon using setTabText()/setTabIcon(). A tab page can remove with removeTab().

Top-Level and Child Widgets

A widget is always an independent window (top-level widget). For these widgets, setWindowTitle() and setWindowIcon() set the title bar and icon respectively.

Non-window widgets are child widgets displayed within their parent widgets. Most widgets in Qt are mainly helpful as child widgets. For example, showing a button as a top-level window is possible, but most people prefer to put their buttons inside other widgets, such as QDialog.

QDialog

A dialog window is always a top window used for short-term tasks and brief communications with the user. It may be modal or modeless, provide a return value, and have default buttons. It can also have a QSizeGrip in its lower-right corner, using setSizeGripEnabled().

Note that QDialog (and any other widget with type Qt::Dialog) uses the parent widget differently from other classes. A dialog is a top-level widget, but its default location is centered on the parent's top-level widget if it has a parent.

The QWidget::setParent() function change the ownership of widget. The function allows explicitly setting the reparented widget's window flags; using the overloaded function, clear the window flags specifying the window-system properties for the widget.

QGroupBox

It widget is used to hold child widgets in a layout by QGridLayout. The QLabel child widgets to indicate their total sizes. If you want to use a QWidget to hold child widgets.

QGridLayout

A group box provides:

- A-frame

- A title on top

- A keyboard shortcut

- Displays various other widgets inside itself

The keyboard shortcut focuses on one of the group box child widgets. It lets you set the title and the title's alignment where group boxes can be checkable. The child widgets in checkable boxes are enabled or disabled depending on whether the group box is checked or not.

You can minimize the space of a group box by enabling the flat property, and in most styles, this property can remove the frame's left, right, and bottom edges.

It doesn't lay out the child widgets. The following example shows how to set up a QGroupBox with a layout:

```
QGroupBox *groupBox = new QGroupBox(tr("Exclusive Radio
Buttons"));
QRadioButton *radio1 = new QRadioButton(tr("&Radio button
1"));
QRadioButton *radio2 = new QRadioButton(tr("R&adio button
2"));
QRadioButton *radio3 = new QRadioButton(tr("Ra&dio button
3"));
radio1->setChecked(true);
QVBoxLayout *vbox = new QVBoxLayout;
vbox->addWidget(radio1);
vbox->addWidget(radio2);
vbox->addWidget(radio3);
vbox->addStretch(1);
groupBox->setLayout(vbox);
```

QGridLayout

It takes the space available to it by the parentWidget(). Divides it into rows and columns puts each widget it manages into the correct cell. Each column has a minimum width and a stretch factor. The minimum width is set by using setColumnMinimumWidth(). The stretch factor is set by using setColumnStretch().

Usually, each widget or layout is put into a cell using addWidget(). A widget can occupy multiple cells using the row and column by addItem() and addWidget(). QGridLayout distributes the size over the columns/rows based on the stretch factors.

To remove a widget from a layout, use removeWidget(). Calling QWidget::hide() also removes the widget from the layout till QWidget::show() is called.

Layout Management

The layout system provides a powerful way of arranging child widgets within a widget that makes good use of the available space.

A set of layout management classes is used to describe how widgets are laid out in an application's user interface. These layouts position and resize widgets when the amount of space available for changes, ensuring that they are arranged and that the user interfaces as a whole remain usable.

All QWidget subclasses use layouts to manage their children. The setLayout() function applies a layout. When a layout is set on, a widget takes charge of the following tasks:

- Positioning of child widgets

- Sensible default sizes for windows and minimum sizes for windows

- Resize handling and automatic updates when contents change

Qt's Layout Classes

Qt's layout classes were designed for hand-written C++ code, allowing measurements to be specified in pixels for simplicity, making them easy to understand and use. The code generated for forms created using Qt Designer also uses the layout classes. Qt Designer is helpful when experimenting with the design of a form since it avoids the compile, link, and run cycle usually involved in user interface development.

1. QBoxLayout

2. QButtonGroup

3. QFormLayout

4. QGraphicsAnchor

5. QGraphicsAnchorLayout

6. QGridLayout

7. QGroupBox

8. QHBoxLayout

9. QLayout

10. QLayoutItem

11. QSizePolicy

12. QSpacerItem

13. QStackedLayout

14. QStackedWidget

15. QVBoxLayout

16. QWidgetItem

Let's discuss each of them in detail.

1. **QBoxLayout**

It takes the space from its parent layout or the parentWidget(), divides it into a row of boxes, makes each managed widget fill one box.

Horizontal box layout with five child widgets

When the QBoxLayout's orientation is Qt::Horizontal, the boxes are placed in a row with given sizes. Each widget gets at least its minimum and maximum sizes.

Vertical box layout with five child widgets

When the QBoxLayout's orientation is Qt::Vertical, the boxes are placed in a column with given sizes.

The way to create a QBoxLayout is to use classes such as QHBoxLayout (for Qt::Horizontal boxes) or QVBoxLayout (for Qt::Vertical boxes). You can use the QBoxLayout directly, specifying its direction as LeftToRight, RightToLeft, TopToBottom, or BottomToTop.

If the QBoxLayout is not the top-level layout, you must add it to its parent layout before doing anything with it. The way to add a layout is by calling parentLayout->addLayout().

You can add boxes using one of four functions:

- addWidget() is used to add a widget to the QBoxLayout and set the widget's stretch factor.

Syntax:

```
void QBoxLayout::addWidget(QWidget *widget, int
stretch = 0, Qt::Alignment alignment =
Qt::Alignment())
```

It can add a widget to the end of this box layout, with a stretch factor of stretch and alignment.

The stretch factor applies in the direction of the QBoxLayout and relative to the other boxes and widgets in the QBoxLayout.

Suppose the stretch factor is 0 and nothing else in the QBoxLayout has a stretch factor more significant than zero. In that case, the space is distributed according to the QWidget:sizePolicy() of each widget involved.

The alignment is specified by alignment. The default alignment is 0, which means the widget fills the entire cell.

- addSpacing() is used to create an empty box; this is one of your functions to create lovely and spacious dialogs. See below for ways to set margins.

Syntax:

```
void QBoxLayout::addSpacing(int size)
```

It can add a non-stretchable space with size to the end of this box layout. QBoxLayout provides default margin and spacing. This function adds additional space.

- addStretch() is used to create an empty, stretchable box.

Syntax:

```
void QBoxLayout::addStretch(int stretch = 0)
```

It can add a stretchable space with zero minimum size and stretch factor stretch to the end of this box layout.

- addLayout() is used to add a box containing another QLayout to the row and set that layout's stretch factor.

Syntax:

```
void QBoxLayout::addStrut(int size)
```

Limits the perpendicular dimension of the box example, height if the box is left to right, to a minimum of size. Other constraints may increase the limit.

You can use insertWidget(), insertSpacing(), insertStretch(), or insertLayout() to insert a box at a particular position in the layout.

It can also include two margin widths:

- **setContentsMargins()**
  It can set the width of the outer border on each side of the widget and reserve space for each of the QBoxLayout's four sides.

```
setSpacing()
```

It sets the width between neighboring boxes. The style provides the margin default. The default margin is 9 for child widgets and 11 for windows. To remove a widget from a layout, use remove-Widget(). Calling this QWidget::hide() on a widget also removes the widget from the layout.

2. **QBoxLayout::Direction**

This type is used to determine the direction of a box layout.

Constant	Description
QBoxLayout::LeftToRight	Horizontal from left to right.
QBoxLayout::RightToLeft	Horizontal from right to left.
QBoxLayout::TopToBottom	Vertical from top to bottom.
QBoxLayout::BottomToTop	Vertical from bottom to top.

3. **QFormLayout Class**

It is a convenience class that lays out the children in a two-column form, and the left column consists of labels, whereas the right column consists of "field"" widgets such as line editors, spin boxes, etc.

It is a higher level that provides the following advantages:

- Adherence to the different platform's guidelines.

- Support for wrapping long rows.

- Convenient API for creating label-field pairs.

4. **QGraphicsAnchorLayout Class**

It allows developers to specify how widgets should be placed relative to each other and the layout itself. The specification is made by adding anchors to the layout by calling addAnchor(), addAnchors(), or addCornerAnchors().

The anchor() function can access existing anchors in the layout can be accessed with the anchor() function. Items that are anchored are automatically added to the layout, and if items are removed, all their anchors will be automatically removed.

We are using an anchor layout to align simple colored widgets. Anchors are always set up between edges of an item, where the "center" is also considered to be an edge. Consider the following example:

```
layout->addAnchor(b, Qt::AnchorLeft, a, Qt::AnchorRight);
layout->addAnchor(b, Qt::AnchorTop, a, Qt::AnchorBottom);
```

5. **QGridLayout Class**

   It is made available to it by the parentWidget(), divides it into rows and columns, puts each widget managed into the correct cell. Columns and rows behave identically, but rows have equivalent functions.

   Each column has a minimum width, and the minimum width is set using setColumnMinimumWidth(). The stretch factor is set using setColumnStretch(), which determines how much of the available space.

6. **QGroupBox Class**

   A group box provides:

   - A frame

   - A title on top

   - A keyboard shortcut

   - Displays various other widgets inside itself

   The keyboard shortcut focuses on one of the group box's children widgets.

   It also lets you set the title and the title's alignment. Group boxes can be checkable. Child widgets in checkable group boxes are enabled or disabled depending on the group box is checked or not.

   You can minimize the space of a group box by enabling the flat property, and in most styles, this property can remove the frame's left, right, and bottom edges.

   QGroupBox doesn't automatically layout the child widgets (often QCheckBoxes or QRadioButtons but can be any widgets). The example shows how to set up a QGroupBox with a layout.

   Example of QGroupBox:

```
QGroupBox *groupBox = new QGroupBox(tr("Exclusive
Radio Buttons"));

QRadioButton *radio1 = new QRadioButton(tr("&Radio
button 1"));
QRadioButton *radio2 = new QRadioButton(tr("R&adio
button 2"));
QRadioButton *radio3 = new QRadioButton(tr("Ra&dio
button 3"));

radio1->setChecked(true);
```

```
QVBoxLayout *vbox = new QVBoxLayout;
vbox->addWidget(radio1);
vbox->addWidget(radio2);
vbox->addWidget(radio3);
vbox->addStretch(1);
groupBox->setLayout(vbox);
```

7. **QHBoxLayout Class**

It is used to construct horizontal box layout objects. The use of the class is like given below.

```
QWidget *window = new QWidget;
QPushButton *button1 = new QPushButton("One");
QPushButton *button2 = new QPushButton("Two");


QHBoxLayout *layout = new QHBoxLayout(window);
layout->addWidget(button1);
layout->addWidget(button2);
window->show();
```

First, we create the widgets to add to the layout. Then, we make the QHBoxLayout object, setting the window as a parent by passing in the constructor. Next, add the widgets to the layout. The window will be the parent of the widgets added to the layout.

If you don't pass the parent window in the constructor, you can use QWidget::setLayout() to install the QHBoxLayout object onto the window.

8. **QVBoxLayout Class**

QVBoxLayout Class is used to construct vertical box layout objects.

The use of the class is like given below:

```
QWidget *window = new QWidget;
QPushButton *button1 = new QPushButton("One");
QPushButton *button2 = new QPushButton("Two");
QVBoxLayout *layout = new QVBoxLayout(window);
layout->addWidget(button1);
layout->addWidget(button2);
window->show();
```

First, create the widgets to add to the layout. Then, we make the QVBoxLayout object, setting the window as a parent by passing it in the constructor. Now add the widgets to the layout. The window will be the parent of the widgets added to the layout.

If you don't pass the parent window in the constructor, you can use QWidget::setLayout() to install the QVBoxLayout object onto the window.

Horizontal, Vertical, Grid, and Form Layouts

The way to give widgets a good layout is to use the built-in layout managers:

- QHBoxLayout

- QVBoxLayout

- QGridLayout

- QFormLayout

These classes inherit from QLayout, which derives from QObject. To create more complex layouts, you can use nest layout managers inside each other.

- A QHBoxLayout lays widgets in a horizontal row, from left to right (or right to left for right-to-left languages).

- A QVBoxLayout lays widgets in a vertical column-like from top to bottom.

- A QGridLayout lays widgets in a 2-dimensional grid. Widgets can get multiple cells.

- A QFormLayout lays widgets in a 2-column descriptive label-field style.

Styles and Style Aware Widgets

The QStyle class is a base class that can encapsulate a GUI's look. Qt's built-in widgets use to perform all of their drawings, ensuring that they look like the equivalent native widgets.

Qt programming comes with built-in styles. Certain styles are available on specific platforms. Some custom styles are available as plugins or by creating an instance of a particular style class using QStyleFactory::create() and setting it with QApplication::setStyle().

QProxyStyle Class

A QProxyStyle wraps a QStyle for dynamically overriding painting or other specific style behavior.

The QStyle Implementation

The QStyle contains functions to draw the widgets, static helper functions to do tasks, and functions to do the various calculations while drawing. The style helps widgets with the layout of the contents. Moreover, it creates a QPalette containing QBrushes to draw with.

It draws graphical elements such as a widget or a widget like a push-button, a window frame, a scroll bar. Most draw functions take four arguments:

- a QWidget on which the drawing is going to be performed

- an enum value that specifies which graphical element to draw

- a QStyleOption that specifies how and where to render that element

- a QPainter that used to draw the element

When a widget style to draw an element, it provides the style with a QStyleOption, a class containing the information for drawing. It is possible to make draw widgets without connecting in any code for any widget.

Customizing a Style

Inherit QProxyStyle virtual methods to customize an existing style. QProxyStyle allows one to specify a particular base style or automatically use the application style when it is left unspecified. The former controls the base style and works best if the customization expects a specific behavior. In contrast, the latter provides a platform-agnostic way to customize the application style that defaults to the native platform style.

Implementing a Custom Style

QCommonStyle provides a convenient base for full custom-style implementations. The approach is the same as QProxyStyle but inherits QCommonStyle appropriate virtual methods. We give a walkthrough of how to style individual Qt widgets also examine the QStyle virtual functions, member variables, and enumerations.

Classes for Widget Styling

These classes are used to customize the appearance and style.

- QColor

QColor Class

Color is specified in RGB means red, green, and blue components. Still, it is also possible to define it in terms of HSV, which is hue, saturation, and value, and CMYK, which is cyan, magenta, yellow, and black components. Color can also specify using a color name.

The QColor creates the color based on RGB values, HSV or CMYK values, Hsv(), and toCmyk() functions. These can return a copy of the color by using the format. The static fromRgb(), fromHsv(), and fromCmyk() functions colors from the specified values. A color can convert to any of the three formats using the convertTo(), or any of the setRgb(), setHsv(), and setCmyk() function. The spec() function tells how the color was specified.

A color can set by passing an RGB string or an ARGB string or a color name to the setNamedColor() function. The name() function can returns the name of the color in the format "#RRGGBB." Colors can set by using setRgb(), setHsv(), and setCmyk(). Use the lighter() and darker() functions to get a lighter or darker color respectively.

Integer vs. Floating Point Precision

QColor supports floating-point precision and provides floating-point versions of all the color components functions, for example, getRgbF(), hueF(), and fromCmykF(). The components stored 16-bit integers and minor deviations between the values. For example, setRgbF() and the values return by the getRgbF() function to rounding. While the integer-based functions take values in the range 0–255 (except hue(), which must have values 0–359), the floating-point functions accept values of 0.0–1.0.

Alpha-Blended Drawing

QColor supports alpha-blended outlining and filling. The alpha color specifies the transparency effect, 0 represents a fully transparent color, and 255 denotes a fully opaque color.

- QColorSpace

QColorSpace Class

Color values can interpret in different ways and, based on the interpretation, can live in other spaces. We call these color spaces.

It provides access to creating predefined color spaces and generates QColorTransforms for converting colors from one colorspace to another. It can also represent colorspaces defined ICC profiles or embedded in images that do not fit the predefined color spaces.

Generally, a color space can be conceived as a combination of a set of primary colors and a transfer function. The primaries define the axes of the color space and the transfer function of how values are mapped on the axes. The primaries are represented by three primary colors representing exactly how red, green, and blue look in this particular color space. The white color means where and how bright, pure white is. The color range expressable is called the gamut, and a colorspace representing a more comprehensive range of colors is also known as wide-gamut colorspace.

- QColorTransform

QColorTransform Class

It is a transformation between color spaces. It can apply color and pixels to convert them from one color space to another.

Setting up a QColorTransform takes some preprocessing, so it is recommended to keep around QColorTransforms that you often need instead of generating them on the fly.

- QCommonStyle

QCommonStyle Class

It implements the widget's look familiar to all GUI styles provided by Qt. Since QCommonStyle inherits QStyle, its functions are fully documented in the QStyle documentation.

- QCursor

QCursor Class

The class is used to create mouse cursors associated with particular widgets and to get and set the mouse cursor's position. Qt has several standard cursor shapes. You can make custom cursor shapes based on a QBitmap, a mask, and a hotspot. use QWidget::setCursor() associate a cursor with a widget. use QCursor::setShape() to set a cursor shape. or the QCursor constructor, which takes shape as an argument. You can use predefined cursors in the Qt::CursorShape enum. Use the QCursor constructor to create a cursor with a bitmap, which takes a bitmap and a mask. To set or get the mouse cursor's position, use the static methods QCursor::pos() and QCursor::setPos().

- QFont

QFont Class

It can regard as a query for one or more fonts on the system. When creating a QFont object, specify various attributes the font to have. Qt uses the font with the selected attributes. The attributes of the font that is used are retrievable from a QFontInfo object.

If the system provides an exact match, then precise match() returns true. To get measurements, you can use QFontMetricsF t, e.g., the pixel length of a string using QFontMetrics::width().

Attributes that are not explicitly set will not affect the font selection algorithm, and default values will be preferred instead. Use QRawFont to load a specific physical font.

Create QFonts like given below,

```
QFont serifFont("Times", 10, QFont::Bold);
```

- QFontDatabase

QFontDatabase Class

The common use of the class is to query the database for the list of font families(). the pointSizes(), styles() are available for each family. There is an alternative to pointSizes() is smoothSizes(), which returns the sizes. When you specify a family, you either use the old hyphenated "foundry-family" format or the bracketed "family [foundry]" format.

Example: "Cronyx-Helvetica" or "Helvetica [Cronyx]."

If the family has a foundry, it returns using the bracketed format. The font() returns a QFont given a family, style, and size. A family and style combination can check to see if it is italic() or bold() and to retrieve its weight(). To obtain a text-version of a style, you can use the styleString()

- QFontInfo

QFontInfo Class

It provides the same access functions as QFont. For example, family(), pointSize(), italic(), weight(), fixedPitch(), styleHint(), etc. But the QFont access functions return the values set, a QFontInfo object returns the values that apply to the font used to draw the text.

For example, when the program asks for a 25-pt Courier font on a machine that has a non-scalable 24pt Courier font, QFont will use the 24pt Courier for rendering. In this case, QFont::pointSize() returns 25 and QFontInfo::pointSize() returns 24.

- QGraphicsAnchor

QGraphicsAnchor Class
It provides and enables you to query and manipulate an anchor's properties. When an anchor is added to the layout with GraphicsAnchorLayout::addAnchor(), it returns where the properties are initialized to their default values. The properties can be further changed, and they will be picked up the next time the layout is activated.

- QGraphicsAnchorLayout

- QPalette

- QStyle

- QStyleFactory

- Creates QStyle objects

- QStyleHintReturn

- QStyleHintReturnMask

- QStyleHintReturnVariant

- QStyleOption

- QStylePainter

Language Binding
Although Qt applications are usually written in C++ and QML, bindings to other languages exist. These are not part of Qt but are provided by various third parties. Riverbank Computing, for example, offers commercial and free software Python bindings (PyQt). For more language bindings, see Category: LanguageBindings.

The Qt API is implemented in C++. It provides additional features for cross-platform development. QML introduced with Qt Quick is a

CSS and JavaScript language designed to describe the user interface of a program.

Both what it looks like and how it behaves. Bindings to Qt exist for other languages such as Python, Ring, Go, Rust, PHP, and Java. Officially, the project maintains the Python bindings under the name of Qt for Python.

Here is the complete list of the Qt language binding:

1. C++

2. C

3. C#

4. Crystal

5. D

6. Go

7. Haskell

8. Javascript

9. Java

10. Lua Pascal

11. Python

12. Julia

13. QML

14. Rust

15. Scheme

16. Ring

17. Ruby

18. Zig

C++ Development with Qt

Qt is a C++ toolkit with an extension for QML and Javascript. There exist many language bindings for Qt, but as Qt is developed in C++, the spirit of C++ can be found throughout the classes. In this section, we will look at

Qt from a C++ perspective to better understand how to extend QML with native plugins developed using C++. Through C++, it is possible to grow and control the execution environment provided to QML.

Qt provides an intuitive C++ class library with a rich set of application build blocks for C++ development. Qt goes beyond C++ in inter-object communication and flexibility for advanced GUI development. Qt adds the following features to C++:

- A powerful mechanism for inter-object communication called signals and slots.

- Queryable and designable object properties.

- Powerful events and events filters.

- Contextual use string translation for internationalization.

- Sophisticated interval drove timers that make it possible to integrate many tasks in an event-driven GUI elegantly.

- Guarded pointers are automatically set to 0 when the referenced object is destroyed, unlike standard C++ tips, which become dangling pointers when their things are destroyed.

- A dynamic cast works across library boundaries.

Python Development with Qt

PyQt is a GUI widgets toolkit. It is a Python interface for Qt, a popular cross-platform GUI library. It is a blend of Python language and the Qt library. This section will assist you in creating graphical applications with the help of PyQt.

It is a set of modules containing many classes and functions. While the QtCore module contains non-GUI functionality for working with files and directories, the QtGui module contains all the graphical controls. There are modules for working with XML (Qt Xml), SVG (Qt Svg), SQL (Qt SQL), etc.

Creating a simple GUI application by using PyQt involves the following steps:

- Firstly, import the QtGui module.

- Create an application object.

- A QWidget object creates the top-level window. Add QLabel object in it.

- Set the caption of the label as "hello world."

- Define the size and position of the window by the setGeometry() method.

- Enter the main loop of the application by the app.exec_() method.

Here is the simple example of Qt programming in Python,

```
import sys
from PyQt4 import QtGui

def window():
    app = QtGui.QApplication(sys.argv)
    w = QtGui.QWidget()
    b = QtGui.QLabel(w)
    b.setText("Qt programming with Python API!")
    w.setGeometry(100,150,100,150)
    b.move(50,20)
    w.setWindowTitle("PyQt")
    w.show()
    sys.exit(app.exec_())

if __name__ == '__main__':
    window()
```

PyQt API is an extensive collection of classes and methods. These classes are defined in 20+ modules. The following are some of the frequently used modules:

- **QtCore:** It is a Core non-GUI class used by other modules.

- **QtGui:** It is a GUI component.

- **QtMultimedia:** It is a class for low-level multimedia programming.

- **QtNetwork:** It is a class for network programming.

- **QtOpenGL:** OpenGL support classes.

- **QtScript:** It is a class for evaluating Qt scripts.

- **QtSql:** Classes for database integration using SQ.

- **QtSvg:** It is a class for displaying the contents of SVG files.

- **QtWebKit:** It is a class for rendering and editing HTML.

- **QtXml:** It is a class for handling XML.

- **QtAssistant:** It supports online help.

- **QtDesigner:** It is a class for extending Qt Designer.

PyQt API contains 400+ classes. The QObject class is the top of the class hierarchy and the base class of all Qt objects. QPaintDevice class is the class for all things that can be painted.

QApplication class manages the main settings and controls flow of a GUI application. It contains the main event loop inside, which window elements generate events. It also handles system-wide and application-wide settings.

QWidget class, derived from QObject and QPaintDevice classes, is the base class for all user interface objects. QDialog and QFrame classes are also derived from QWidget class.

Here is a list of used widgets given below that are the commonly used Widgets:

- **QLabel:** It is used to display text or images.

- **QLineEdit:** It allows the user to enter one line of text.

- **QTextEdit:** It allows the user to enter multiline text.

- **QPushButton:** A command button to invoke action.

- **QRadioButton:** It enables one to choose one from multiple options.

- **QCheckBox:** It enables the choice of more than one option.

- **QSpinBox:** It enables to increase/decrease an integer value.

- **QScrollBar:** It enables access to the contents of a widget beyond the display aperture.

- **QSlider:** It enables to change the bound value linearly.

- **QComboBox:** It provides a dropdown list of items to select from.

- **QMenuBar:** It is a horizontal bar holding QMenu objects.

- **QStatusBar:** It is usually at the bottom of QMainWindow, provides status information.

- **QToolBar:** It is usually at the top of QMainWindow or floating. Contains action buttons.

- **QListView:** It provides a selectable list of items in ListMode or IconMode.

- **QPixmap:** It is an off-screen image representation for display on QLabel or QPushButton object.

- **QDialog:** It is a modal or modeless window that can return information to the parent window.

The PyQt installer comes with a GUI builder tool called Qt Designer. Using its simple drag and drop interface, a GUI interface can be quickly built without writing the code. It is, however, not an IDE such as Visual Studio. Hence, Qt Designer does not have the facility to debug and build the application.

Signals and Slots

Unlike a console mode application executed sequentially, a GUI-based application is event-driven. Functions or methods are performed in response to the user's actions like clicking on a button, selecting an item, or a mouse click.

Widgets are used to build the GUI interface as the source of events. Each PyQt widget, derived from the QObject class, is designed to emit a "signal" in response to several occasions. The signal on its does not perform any action. Instead, it is "connected" to a "slot."

Layout Management

A GUI widget can place inside the container window by specifying its absolute coordinates measured in pixels. The coordinates are relative to the window's dimensions defined by the setGeometry() method.

Here is the syntax of setGeometry(),

```
QWidget.setGeometry(xpos, ypos, width, height)
```

QDialog Class

A QDialog widget presents a top-level window mainly used to collect responses from the user. It can be configured to be Modal or Modeless is the dialog window that can be bypassed).

PyQt API has several preconfigured Dialog widgets such as InputDialog, FileDialog, FontDialog, etc.

QMessageBox

QMessageBox is a commonly used modal dialog to display some informational message and optionally ask the user to respond by clicking any of the standard buttons. Each standard button has a predefined caption role and returns a predefined hexadecimal number.

- **setIcon()**: It displays a predefined icon corresponding to the severity of the message.

- **setText()**: It sets the text of the main message to be displayed.

- **setInformativeText()**: It displays additional information.

- **setDetailText()**: It is dialog shows a Details button. This text appears on clicking it.

- **setTitle()**: It displays the custom title of the dialog.

- **setStandardButtons()**: Here is the list of standard buttons to be displayed. Each button is associated with:

  1. QMessageBox.Ok 0x00000400

  2. QMessageBox.Open 0x00002000

  3. QMessageBox.Save 0x00000800

  4. QMessageBox.Cancel 0x00400000

  5. QMessageBox.Close 0x00200000

  6. QMessageBox.Yes 0x00004000

  7. QMessageBox.No 0x00010000

  8. QMessageBox.Abort 0x00040000

  9. QMessageBox.Retry 0x00080000

  10. QMessageBox.Ignore 0x00100000

- **setDefaultButton()**: It sets the button as default. It emits the clicked signal if Enter is pressed.

- **setEscapeButton()**: It sets the button to be treated as clicked if the escape key is pressed.

KDE FRAMEWORKS

It is a collection of libraries available to Qt-based software stacks on multiple operating systems. It frequently required functionality solutions like hardware integration, file format support, and additional graphical elements. The collection serves as a technological foundation for KDE Plasma 5 and KDE Gear distributed under the GNU Lesser General Public License (LGPL).

Overview

Now KDE Frameworks are based on Qt 5, which enables more widespread use of QML, a more straightforward JavaScript-based declarative programming language for the design. The graphics engine used by QML allows more user interfaces across different devices. Some source code was shifted from being part of KDE Frameworks 5 to being part of Qt 5.2 later. Since the KDE Software Compilation split into KDE Frameworks 5, Plasma 5, and Applications, KDE Frameworks are released monthly and use git.

Structure

The Frameworks have a structure divided into "categories" and "tiers." The "categories" are defined as runtime dependencies.

- **Components:** The KDE Frameworks bundle has consisted of over 70 packages. These existed as a large package which is called kdelibs. It was split into several individual frameworks, some of which are no longer supported by KDE but were integrated into Qt 5.2.

- **Kirigami:** Kirigami is a QML application framework developed by Marco Martin which enables developers to write applications that run natively on Android, iOS, Windows, Plasma Mobile, and any classic Linux desktop environment without code adjustments.

Various applications use it, for example, Linus Torvalds and Dirk Hohndels scuba diving application Subsurface, the messenger client Banji, the Kaidan messenger, Vvave music player, and the KDE software center Discover.

CHAPTER SUMMARY

In this chapter, we have learned the topic Qt programming for making application in KDE Linux-based distro.

CHAPTER 5

Linux Distributions for KDE Plasma Desktop

IN THIS CHAPTER

- ➤ Kubuntu

- ➤ Manjaro KDE

- ➤ Fedora KDE Plasma Desktop Edition

- ➤ Netrunner

- ➤ Garuda Linux

- ➤ Feren OS

- ➤ Arch Linux installation

- ➤ And more

In the last chapter, we have covered Qt toolkit basics, and discussed KDE as a distro operating system that uses Qt as its GUI toolkit. The Qt Company developed the Qt Project under open source, involving developers and organizations working on advanced Qt. It is available both commercially and open source through GPL 2.0, GPL 3.0, and LGPL 3.0 licenses.

Now, we will be going to cover various KDE-based distros. KDE can be the default desktop environment on different major Linux distributions, including Kubuntu, Manjaro KDE, Fedora KDE Plasma Desktop

DOI: 10.1201/9781003309406-5

Edition, Netrunner, Garuda Linux, Feren OS, Arch Linux, Nitrux, openSUSE, etc.

Despite KDE being the most widely used desktop environment, some Linux distros offer a better implementation of KDE. We have put together a list of the best KDE-based Linux distros on the market.

KUBUNTU

The Ubuntu operating system is an official flavor that uses the KDE Plasma Desktop instead of the GNOME desktop environment. The Ubuntu project Kubuntu uses the underlying system. Each package shares the same repositories as Ubuntu, and it is released on the same schedule as Ubuntu.

It was developed by Canonical Ltd. until 2012 and then directly by Blue Systems. Employees of Blue Systems can contribute to KDE and Debian, and community contributors lead Kubuntu development. During the changeover, Kubuntu retained Ubuntu project servers and existing developers.

"Kubuntu" is a trademark held by Canonical Foundation. It is derived from "Ubuntu," prefixing a K to represent the KDE platform. Kubuntu is built on following a widespread naming convention of prefixing K to the name of software released for use on KDE platforms and the KDE community.

Since Ubuntu is a Bantu term roughly to "humanity," since Bantu involves prefixes to noun classes, it turns out the prefix Ku- having the meaning "toward" in Bemba, it is also a meaningful Bemba word translating to "toward humanity." The same word also takes the meaning of "free" in Kirundi.

History

Kubuntu was come into the market on December 10, 2004 at the Ubuntu Mataro Conference in Mataró, Spain. Canonical Foundation employee Andreas Mueller, from Gnoppix, had the idea to make an Ubuntu KDE variant called as Kubuntu. Chris Halls from the office project and Jonathan Riddell from KDE began volunteering on the newborn project on the same evening.

The Kubuntu team released the first edition on April 8, 2005. K Desktop Environment 3 was the default interface until Kubuntu 8.04 or later. That version included KDE Plasma Desktop as an unsupported option which became the default in the subsequent release, 8.10.

Canonical employee announced the end of Canonical's Kubuntu sponsorship on February 6, 2012. Blue Systems was announced on the Kubuntu official website as the new sponsor on April 10, 2012. Both employed by Canonical to work on Kubuntu as well.

Kubuntu follows the same naming system as Ubuntu, with each release has a codename and a version number based on the month of release and year. Canonical Foundation provides support and security updates for Kubuntu components shared with Ubuntu for 18 months five years in case of long-term support (LTS) versions after release. Both a desktop version and an alternative version for the x86 and AMD64 platforms are available. Its CDs were also available through the ShipIt service.

Kubuntu release is given below.

Kubuntu 5.04 (Hoary Hedgehog)

It is an initial release, including KDE 3.4 and selecting the most useful KDE programs. Some of these are not in the official KDE such as Amarok, Kaffeine, Gwenview, and K3b. Inclusion of update-manager/upgrade-notifier; Kickstart compatibility.

The project announced the preview release for 5.04, known as "Hoary Hedgehog," on March 10, and its final release is scheduled for early April.

The first release was announced recently and scheduled for early April. It uses Ubuntu as a base, but with the KDE as a desktop environment and related packages rather than GNOME. We decided to look at both releases to see how far Ubuntu has come since its inception and see what users could expect in the forthcoming release.

The Ubuntu distribution is based on Debian for those unfamiliar with the project, but with a six-month release schedule, like GNOME and OpenBSD. Releases are supported, meaning critical bug fixes, and security updates, for 18 months. Ubuntu has a bit narrower scope than Debian, however. Ubuntu supports only three architectures, Intel/x86, AMD64, and PowerPC, and has a more limited set of packages (the "main" and "restricted" repositories) to provide updates for. A more extensive package collection is available through the "universe" and "multiverse" repositories.

The release numbers may seem like version inflation, but reflect the year and month of the release, hence 5.04 for Hoary Hedgehog and 4.10 for Warty Warthog – the first Ubuntu release, from October 2004.

To install Kubuntu, we followed the instructions on the Kubuntu official documentation page. After executing "Sudo apt-get install

Kubuntu-desktop" and choosing between KDM and GDM, we installed Kubuntu, the KDE 3.4.0 desktop, and several KDE applications.

Whereas Debian installs a reasonably minimal system and then allows the user to choose packages, Ubuntu and Kubuntu are default applications for desktop use, allowing less experienced users to get right away without deciding which application to use for email, spreadsheets, word processing, or web browsing. For example, Ubuntu installs GNOME 2.10 Thunderbird, OpenOffice.org, Firefox, Totem, Synaptic, Gaim, and the Gimp. Kubuntu installs KDE version 3.4 Konqueror, Kontact, Kopete, Kynaptic, Akregator, and other apps for KDE than most users would want.

Though GNOME and KDE are the default desktop environment for Ubuntu and Kubuntu, respectively, KDE and GNOME are not available desktops to Ubuntu and Kubuntu users. Other desktops are available: XFce, Blackbox, Enlightenment, fvwm, and several other window managers in the Ubuntu Universe repository. This writer prefers the XFce desktop environment and has happily used XFce with Ubuntu.

Kubuntu 5.10 (Breezy Badger)

The Kubuntu project, a subproject of Ubuntu Linux, has announced a preview release of Kubuntu 5.10 "Breezy Badger": "The Kubuntu 5.10 Preview was the beta release for the next version of Kubuntu. In this release is the latest KDE 3.4.2, OpenOffice.org 2 beta 2, X.Org 6.8.2. Other new features include Krita – state-of-the-art bitmap image editor, Katapult – an advanced application and item launcher, System Settings – a user-friendly replacement for KControl, a simplified Konqueror profile." More information about the release can read in the official release announcement.

KDE 3.4.3 and the Guidance configuration tools. It comes with the Adept Package Manager, the first to use web tags for easier searching that replaces the Kynaptic package manager used in the previous release. System Settings, a re-organized kcontrol-like center, KDE Bluetooth; Graphical boot process with progress bar (USplash); OEM Installer Support; Launchpad tracking; GCC 4.0.

6.06 LTS (Dapper Drake)

Rate this project Kubuntu, one of the distributions belonging to the Ubuntu family of Linux operating systems, is the first to publish a formal announcement about the product's new release: "Kubuntu 6.06 LTS has been released. This release comes with KDE version 3.5.2, includes a new installer that you can use directly from the live desktop CD, and is focused on stability and bug fixes. KDE 6.06 was supported for three years on the desktop and five years on the server." Kubuntu 6.06 for three processor architectures and in various configurations is available for download from several mirrors servers, while free CD images can also be ordered from its ShipIt system.

LTS release; Live CD and Installer on one disc; Ubiquity installer; Adept Notifier and Simplified Installer; X Display Configuration from Guidance; Better Asian language support; Avahi networking software.

7.04 (Feisty Fawn)

It is the big release for the Ubuntu family of distributions. Kubuntu is the first to announce the new version: "Kubuntu 7.04 was released is available for download now. Kubuntu 7.04 stepped over the edge, it is becoming the release to date. It has improved desktop, updated applications, and increased usability features are just a few of the surprises with this latest release. The goal for Kubuntu 7.04 was to continue creating a secure and stable environment, working towards the perfect KDE-based operating system. Starting with the base of Ubuntu with implementation of KDE, Kubuntu 7.04 set out to smooth the rough edges and polish of Kubuntu."

KDE 3.5.6; Migration assistant; KVM; Easy codec/restricted drivers installation; System Settings restructured into General and Advanced categories; Improved Hewlett-Packard printer management; KNetworkManager included; WPA support; Topic-based help system; OEM installer update; PowerPC support officially dropped.

7.10 (Gutsy Gibbon)

The Kubuntu project has announced the final release of Kubuntu 7.10: "Kubuntu 7.10 has been released is available for download now. Kubuntu 7.10 removed the feistiness, becoming the gutsiest release to date. It has improved desktop, increased usability features, updated applications are just a few of the surprises with this latest release. The goal for Kubuntu 7.10, code-named Gutsy Gibbon, was to remove the edge and feistiness from previous releases and continue creating a secure and stable desktop environment on the road to becoming the perfect KDE-based operating system."

New background ships with Strigi and Dolphin as default. Qt port of GDebi visual installer for package files. It includes Restricted Drivers Manager for the first time. The New Kubuntu-restricted-extras package is available for download from the repositories.

8.10 (Intrepid Ibex)

KDE version 4.1.2 desktop environment by default Linux, Xserver, Adept Manager, KNetworkManager, KWin desktop effects, various Kubuntu tool integration.

Ubuntu 8.10 desktop is a full-fledged replacement for a Windows desktop that has all the software you need to do things on Windows desktops. The advantages are that you get a secure system without DRM preventions that works on old hardware, do the best thing is: all software comes free of charge.

The Ubuntu desktop to have the following software installed:

- The GIMP
- F-Spot
- Google Picasa
- Firefox
- Opera
- Flash Player 10
- Thunderbird
- Evolution
- aMule
- BitTornado
- Azureus/Vuze
- Pidgin
- Skype
- Google Earth
- Xchat IRC – IRC client
- OpenOffice Writer
- OpenOffice Calc
- Adobe Reader
- GnuCash

- Scribus

- Amarok

- Audacity

- Banshee

- MPlayer

- Rhythmbox Music Player

- gtkPod

- XMMS

- dvd::rip

- Kino

- Sound Juicer CD Extractor

- VLC Media Player

- Helix Player

- Totem

- Xine

- Brasero

- K3B

9.10 (Karmic Koala)

KDE 4.3.2 is a desktop environment by default, and the GRUB 2 system moved to Upstart, kernel 2.6.31.

Kubuntu is made with the latest KDE desktop on a solid Ubuntu core. We believe this combination delivers a fantastic all-around home desktop experience. Our tools and applications will provide you with all you need for most of your tasks, with more available. Whether browsing the web, playing music, composing an email, or connecting with your friends on social networks, Kubuntu 9.10 brings you an innovative and attractive platform for all your desktop needs.

Desktop is the cutting edge KDE 4, and release updates it to another significant version – many changes having bug fixes, new functionality, etc.

10.04 LTS (Lucid Lynx)

By default KDE 4.4.2 desktop environment, kernel version 2.6.32, KPackageKit 0.5.4, Firefox KDE integration, touchpad configuration module by default. Ubuntu 10.04 desktop is a full-fledged replacement for a Windows desktop, i.e., it has all the software that need to do the things on their Windows desktops. Some advantages are clear you get a secure system without DRM restrictions that can work even on old hardware; the best thing is that all software come free of charge. Many security updates will be available for desktops and five years for servers for three years.

10.10 (Maverick Meerkat)

Maverick ships with KDE SC 4.5 installed the most stable and attractive version of the KDE 4 series to date. One tool that has improved is the Ubiquity installer. It is more aesthetically appealing and easier to use than ever, and it gives users the ability to install restricted media features (like MP3 playback support) during initial installation. It is probably as close as they will ever get to include that support within the OS itself.

Maverick Features:

- **New Message Indicator:** When new messages are received, the latest indicator handles them and changes color to inform the user.

- Default browser changed to Rekonq.

- New bluetooth stack.

- Pulseaudio inclusion.

- Global menu for the netbook.

- Combining of the Desktop and Netbook Editions.

- Updated Kpackagekit with categories. Updated Installer.

11.04 (Natty Narwhal)

KDE SC 4.6 is a default environment, kernel 2.6.38, GStreamer multimedia backend for Phonon, GTK Oxygen theme, games in the default install, UDisks, and UPower replace HAL.

The Kubuntu team is to announce the release of 11.04 – codename Natty Narwhal's release, the latest version of our widespread Linux distribution, based on Ubuntu and KDE's Plasma and Applications 4.6. With the combination of its backbone, the amazing KDE Software Compilation, and a few unique extras, 11.04 aims to provide the most satisfactory fusion of stability, beauty, and up-to-date software.

Whether working, browsing the web, playing your music, composing an email, or connecting with your friends on social networks, Kubuntu brings you a powerful, innovative, and attractive platform for all your desktop needs.

12.04 LTS (Precise Pangolin)
The third Kubuntu LTS release uses KDE SC 4.8, kernel 3.2.0. Precise Pangolin's release overviews the release and documents the known issues with Ubuntu 12.04.5 and its flavors. The release notes for 12.04 with its minor updates 12.04.1, 12.04.2, 12.04.3, 12.04.4 are also available.

13.04 (Raring Ringtail)
Kubuntu 13.04 (Raring Ringtail) is an operating system based on various technologies, such as KDE Software, Plasma, Linux kernel, Debian, and Ubuntu.

It is based on KDE SC, so it has nothing to do with the Unity environment used in the regular version of Ubuntu. Therefore, no online searches are being done, either to Canonical services or Amazon. Muon Suite 2, KDE SC 4.10, LibreOffice 4, Homerun launcher, out-of-the-box MTP support.

This distribution is based on KDE Plasma 5 and Applications 4.10.2, which adds a new screen locker, Qt Quick notifications, color correction in Gwenview, and faster indexing in the semantic desktop:

- The Muon Suite for app installation and upgrade has been implemented. It provides the support needed to install Plasma widgets found in KDE's KNewStuff framework from within Software Center and Muon Discover.

- Rekonq 2 is the default browser in the distribution. It has many new features such as inline spellcheck, an incognito mode, a startup option, pinning tabs, and more.

- The Screen Management has been improved. Users will find it easier to attach and unattached extra monitors.

- Oxygen Sans, a new font from KDE's artists, is now available by default.

- The installer has received an upgrade.

14.04 LTS (Trusty Tahr)

KDE SC 4.13.0 is the default environment, LibreOffice 4.2.3.3 is a brand new LTS version with the latest KDE software to enjoy. LTS means bug fixes and security updates will be added for the next five years, so you can safely use it until 2019. New releases of essential KDE Software will also be available from the Kubuntu Updates and Kubuntu Backports PPAs. The default browser changed back to Firefox.

15.04 (Vivid Vervet)

Kubuntu 15.04 is the distribution that uses the Plasma 5 branch, and others will notice the change. If you don't upgrade your system to the latest version of Kubuntu, you will be stuck with the previous iteration from the Plasma 4 branch, which is no longer supported. KDE Plasma 5.2.2 is the default desktop environment. Adaptation to systems and SDDM. Behind-the-scenes work on the change to Wayland.

16.04 LTS (Xenial Xerus)

Ubuntu 16.04 Xenial Xerus with Unity also covered the Mate flavor, and now we have Kubuntu as the next subject. Like the Mate and other flavors, Kubuntu will be getting a three years of LTS support, after which they won't get updated. Still, the underlying Ubuntu base will be continually supported until the expiration of the five-year period, which only applies to the original Ubuntu.

Kubuntu 16.04 ships will fly the KDE 5.5 desktop environment, which is disappointing as the newest KDE release is at 5.6, many other distros using the KDE desktop environment have adopted this update.

17.04 (Zesty Zapus)

This version has been codenamed "Zesty Zapus," Kubuntu 17.04 continues our proud tradition of integrating the latest and most remarkable open source technologies into a high-quality, easy-to-use, introducing new features and fixing bug Linux distribution.

There have been updates to core packages, including a new 4.10-based kernel, Plasma 5.9.4, KDE Frameworks 5.31, KDE Applications 16.12.3.

The Kubuntu desktop had some exciting improvements, with newer versions of Qt, updates to other major packages like Krita, Kdenlive, Firefox, and LibreOffice, and stability improvements to the Plasma desktop environment.

18.04 LTS (Bionic Beaver)

The Kubuntu 18.04 LTS has been released, featuring the beautiful KDE Plasma 5.12 LTS: simple by default, powerful when needed.

Codenamed "Bionic Beaver," Kubuntu 18.04 continues our tradition of giving you Friendly Computing by integrating the latest and most remarkable open source technologies into a high-quality, easy-to-use Linux distribution.

There have been updates to core packages, including a new 4.15-based kernel, KDE Frameworks 5.44, Plasma 5.12 LTS, and KDE Applications 17.12.3.

19.04 (Disco Dingo)

Kubuntu 19.04 was released on April 18, 2019, based on Ubuntu 19.04, and was available for desktop/laptop computers. This release was preceded by version 18.10. Compared to previous Kubuntu releases, this version includes some new updates, such as Linux Kernel 5.0, KDE Plasma 5.15.4, KDE Apps 18.12.3, KDE Frameworks 5.56, LibreOffice 6.2.2, Firefox 66, Qt 5.12, and more.

Kubuntu 19.04 supported for nine months till January 2020.

KDE Applications 18.12.3, KDE Frameworks 5.56, Qt 5.12.2, Linux Kernel 5.0, LibreOffice 6.2.2, Firefox 66, KDE Connect 1.3.4, KDevelop 5.3.2, Krita 4.1.7, Latte Dock 0.8.8.

20.04 LTS (Focal Fossa)

Kubuntu 20.04.2 LTS was released on February 4, 2021, based on Ubuntu 20.04.2 LTS and was available for desktop/laptop computers. This release was preceded by version 20.04. Kubuntu 20.04.2 didn't support 32-bit CPU architecture and only installed 64-bit versions. Compared to previous Kubuntu releases, this version includes bug fixes, app updates, performance tweaks, security updates, and more.

Kubuntu 20.04.1 LTS (Focal Fossa) was released on August 6, 2020, based on Ubuntu 20.04.1 LTS and was available for desktop/laptop computers. This release was preceded by version 20.04. Kubuntu 20.04.1 didn't support 32-bit CPU architecture and only installed 64-bit versions. Compared to previous Kubuntu releases, this version includes bug fixes, app updates, performance tweaks, security updates, and more.

Kubuntu 20.04 LTS is the LTS release supported for three years until April 2023. KDE Frameworks 5.68.0, Qt 5.12.8, Linux Kernel 5.4, LibreOffice 6.4.2.2, Firefox 75.

21.04 (Hirsute Hippo)

Kubuntu 21.04 was released on April 22, 2021, based on Ubuntu 21.04, and was available for desktop/laptop computers. This release was preceded by version 20.04. Kubuntu 21.04 didn't support 32-bit CPU architecture and only installed 64-bit versions. Compared to previous Kubuntu releases, this version includes new features and updates such as KDE Plasma 5.21, KDE Framework 5.80, KDE Release Service Application 20.12.3, Kernel 5.11, Firefox 87, LibreOffice 7.1, Qt 5.15.2, Krita 4.4.3, Kdevelop 5.6.2, etc.

Key Highlights:

- It is an Ubuntu-based desktop-focused Linux distro.

- It offers both LTS and non-LTS versions.

- Have good hardware compatibility.

It should be an excellent distro for Linux desktop if the KDE software suite is not your focus.

Kubuntu distro is an official flavor of Ubuntu that provides three years of updates for its LTS editions. Unlike other KDE Neon, you can get better support for various applications limited to KDE software.

You get the various options to opt for an LTS edition or a non-LTS version to get the latest Ubuntu features.

It has improved hardware compatibility compared with other KDE-based distros. It powers a variety of devices that include Kubuntu Focus, Slimbook. The hardware compatibility is something you can rely on.

MANJARO KDE

The edition is supported by the Manjaro and comes with KDE Plasma, a very modern and flexible desktop. It is a distro based on Arch Linux its installation and configuration. The Manjaro KDE version is configured to use KDE Plasma and core applications. KDE Plasma is now the default desktop environment of Manjaro Linux.

KDE Plasma is for those who want a user-friendly and customizable desktop. It is a feature-rich and flexible desktop environment that provides several menu styles to access applications. An incredible built-in interface to efficiently access and install new themes, widgets, etc. from the Internet is also worth. KDE Plasma is by default a clean work area for real-world usage that intends to stay out of your way, so the user can create the workflow that makes it more effective to complete tasks.

Key Highlights:

- It is an Arch-based Linux distro.

- It has rolling-release updates.

- It presents a slight learning curve to new Linux users.

- An Arch-Linux-based distribution makes it easy to use Arch as a desktop Linux platform.

It follows a rolling-release schedule that should help you get the latest packages without worrying about the software update period.

Manjaro Is Arch Linux Made Easy

When you burn a LIVE CD or USB, it will make sense to you. A Linux newbie can easily use Manjaro as his first Linux distro, but the same cannot be said about Arch Linux.

The Manjaro team has entirely made Arch Linux available to everyone, newbie or professional, because it carries all the good features in Arch with it; more people can use and access the awesomeness of Arch Linux through Manjaro.

No More PPAs

Manjaro Linux boasts a customized repository that ensures that all accessible software packages, whether updates, fixes, or applications, are thoroughly tested to be stable and compatible with your system. Manjaro's repo is a lot organized, with fewer broken and outdated packages, making it more reliable to use.

The Arch Wiki

The Arch wiki contains documentation for virtually any task you want to complete in Arch Linux and other distributions. Manjaro Linux is an Arch Linux that stays to the heart of Arch, you can take advantage of this elegant knowledge base.

Easy Kernel Switching

Currently, its users can easily switch between using any Linux kernel versions from 3.10 to 4.18 directly from the Kernel section of the Manjaro

Settings Manager. Here, you can recommend Kernel version to use, manage all the present kernels for installation, view their changelogs and type (LTS versions).

Easy Access to Software

An additional bonus, besides the fact that Manjaro uses the AUR, is that many software that are more or less tricky or tedious to install on other distros are readily available for Manjaro users.

For example, all the time Ubuntu users struggled to set up steam and Spotify on their machines, Arch users were chilling.

KDE Neon is the official Linux distribution that features the latest KDE Plasma Desktop, KDE Framework, and KDE Applications from KDE Community. This Linux distribution directly comes from the KDE Development team and is based in Ubuntu. KDE Neon comes with two variants: a User edition and a Developer edition. The User edition is for everyone who wants to experience the latest from the KDE Plasma Desktop tested and ready to use. But it may have some minor bugs – but not a dealbreaker. The Developer edition for, as it says – for developers with cutting-edge packages. It is ideal for those who are a little experienced in the Linux platform and have time to get around occasional problems. But this is also reasonably stable.

Pros:

- It has the latest KDE Applications, Packages, and Frameworks.
- It is based on an Ubuntu base.
- It firsts to receive new KDE Plasma Versions.

Cons:

- It may contain occasional bugs.

FEDORA KDE PLASMA DESKTOP EDITION

The Fedora KDE Plasma DE is a robust Fedora-based operating system utilizing the KDE Plasma Desktop as the primary user interface.

It comes with multiple pre-selected top-quality applications that suit all modern desktop use cases – from online communication like web browsing, instant messaging, electronic mail, through multimedia and entertainment, to an advanced productivity suite, including office applications, and enterprise-grade personal information management.

All KDE applications are integrated with a similar look and feel and an easy-to-use interface, accompanied by an outstanding graphical appearance.

Install KDE Plasma Desktop Environment on Fedora

KDE Plasma is the most customizable Linux Desktop Environment in existence. The KDE Community has developed many high-quality applications that fit users' Desktop needs. The top typical Desktop Applications that come with KDE Plasma include:

- Dolphin file manager

- Kate text editor

- Konqueror web browser

- Kget download manager

- KMail email client

- Krita creative sketching and painting tool

- KDE connect

- Okular document viewer

- KMyMoney personal finance tool

- Kdenlive video editing application

- Amarok music management application

- DigiKam photo management application

Install KDE Plasma on Fedora

KDE Plasma installation on Fedora is an easy process that doesn't require an experienced Linux user. You need to run the following commands on your desktop as a user with Sudo privileges:

```
$ sudo dnf -y group install "KDE Plasma Workspaces."
```

The installation has a list of dependencies that need to be installed.

Switch to KDE Environment on Fedora at Login

Now, reboot your system and select the KDE desktop environment on the Login screen.

```
$ Sudo reboot
```

It should work for Fedora Workstation installations. Click the "settings" icon "Sign In" button.

Key Highlights:

- A unique KDE-based Linux distribution.

- It tailored for workstations and servers.

- It may not be convenient for new Linux users.

- Its hardware compatibility can be an issue.

- It is an independent distribution not based on Ubuntu/Arch upstream Red Hat Enterprise Linux.

Pros:

- It is a well-designed and stable Linux distribution.

- Latest KDE Plasma releases twice a year.

- Suitable for new and advanced users.

- It supports versatile community.

Cons:

- Fedora Linux with KDE may feel a little complex for absolute new Linux users.

NETRUNNER

It is a \Linux Operating System for all PCs, laptops/netbooks, and ARM microcomputers, which only uses the KDE Plasma Desktop environment.

It is a free operating system for desktop computers, laptops or netbooks, and arm-based device-types like the Odroid C1 microcomputer or the Pinebook. It comes in two versions: Netrunner and Netrunner Core, both based on Debian Stable. The Core versions feature KDE Plasma plus a minimal selection of applications, multimedia codecs, and Firefox browser plugins.

Netrunner is a Debian-based distribution featuring a customized KDE desktop with different applications, multimedia codecs, Flash and Java plugins, a unique look and feel. Its modifications are designed to enhance the user-friendliness of the environment while preserving the freedom to tweak. A separate "Rolling" edition, based on Manjaro Linux, was launched in 2014, was discontinued, relaunched in 2017, and discontinued again in 2019. The version available is a Desktop and Core version.

Default software: Among all the default software of Netrunner Desktop are many applications such as:

- Support KDE Plasma Desktop

- Mozilla Firefox (includes Plasma integration)

- Mozilla Thunderbird (includes Plasma integration)

- VLC media player

- LibreOffice

- GIMP

- Krita

- Gwenview

- Kdenlive

- Inkscape

- Samba Mounter (easy NAS setup)

- Steam

- VirtualBox

Here is the complete list of version of KDE in Netrunner.

Netrunner Desktop 21.01

The Netrunner release of Netrunner 21.01 "XOXO" – 64bit ISO. The version is based on the current Debian Stable 10.7 (named buster) and comes with better modern hardware support thanks to Linux Kernel 5.9.15 from Debian

Buster Backports. The Debian Buster (stable version) 10.3-based distro is being dubbed in "Twenty." Netrunner version 20.01 is using KDE Plasma 5.14.5.

Updated packages:

- Netrunner 21.01 ships with all the security updates provided by the Debian system and a new beautiful wallpaper showing the new Codename of this release.

- With the activated Debian Buster repository, we provide updated firmware for using Wi-Fi and Ethernet chips and improved printer drivers to allow more modern hardware support.

- Firefox-ESR and Thunderbird were updated to the stable LTS versions, which get regular security updates provided by Debian security.

- Netrunner maintains its gorgeous look and feels from the previous version based on Breeze Window decoration and the cursor's red colors.

Netrunner Desktop 20.01

The Netrunner immediate availability of Netrunner 20.01 "Twenty" – 64bit ISO. This version marks the 20th release of Netrunner Desktop for Debian/Ubuntu and its 10th year since Netrunner started back in 2010. It is based upon the Debian Stable 10.3 ("buster"), including all updates since the previous release.

After introducing the red cursor and Indigo theme in the last Netrunner 19.08 release, its 20.01 switches to the Breeze Window with polished "Indigo" theme, marking ten years of Netrunner and the 20th release of desktop OS.

Its 20.01 includes the latest LTS version of Plasma 5.14.5 environment, Firefox-ESR, Thunderbird. In addition to the latest Debian 10 stable, its version 20.01 provides the latest security updates with bug fixes.

You can enjoy the preinstalled terminal emulator, Yakuake. However, it comes with a default Konsole terminal.

There are two flavors of Netrunner: the first one is based on Debian and the other on Manjaro/Arch. Both these versions have KDE Plasma as their desktop environment.

Netrunner Desktop 19.08

Netrunner 19.08 has to offer as it also comes with KDE Plasma 5.14.5, Qt 5.11.3, KDE Frameworks 5.54, KDE Applications 18.08, and Thunderbird

60.7.2. Also, the developers have updated its kernel to Linux Kernel 4.19.0~5 as well.

Another change worth mentioning is that this update replaces the regular Firefox with Firefox-ESR (version 60.8.1), which provides long-term stability; all thanks to Debian's security updates.

Netrunner 19.01

It is known as "Blackbird" that release includes the KDE Plasma 5.14.3 desktop environment, the KDE Frameworks 5.51, and Applications 18.08 software, Qt 5.11.3 Mozilla Firefox 64.0 is web browser, Mozilla Thunderbird 60.3 email client, the Krita 4.1.1 painting software.

Its version 19.01 is powered by the Linux 4.19.0 kernel. Last but not least, this release unifies all of the settings and UI-related KCM modules under the main section called "Plasma Tweaks," accessible using the side-bar layout.

Netrunner is an operating system for desktop computers, netbooks, ARM microcomputers, and uses the Plasma desktop environment. The desktop version works with a complete set of preinstalled software for daily. Its core version allows to build up your system or run it on low-spec hardware like arm-boards. Its rolling release is based on Arch/Manjaro, whereas Netrunner Desktop and Core are both Debian-based. Netrunner uses KDE Plasma and tunes it to be as snappy and responsive as possible. We actively sponsor the development of Plasma's core, and new components are included in Netrunner early on, for example:

- Simple menu and Dash

- Task-Manager with Expanding Icons

- Desktop Workspace icons on a desktop, no overlays

- Hot-Spot "Show Desktop" in the lower right corner

- Auto-started KWallet

- Simplified System Settings

- Firefox-ESR and Thunderbird with Plasma Integration

- It has a unified look for KDE and non-KDE-applications via GTK-Configuration

Minimum System Requirements:

- The system has CPU 1.6-GHz Intel Atom

- RAM should be 1GB

- Support Hard Drive Size 15GB

Video Memory 128MB:

- Graphics Card Intel GMA 945

If you want to try Netrunner on VirtualBox, you should allocate 1.5 GB of RAM. Netrunner 18.03 was released. This version builds on Debian's Testing branch and includes the Plasma kernel 5.12 LTS, Linux kernel version 4.14, LibreOffice 6, and Firefox 58.

Netrunner 17.10

It ships with an upgraded stack of KDE Plasma, Frameworks, Apps on an updated Debian Testing, plus the usual selection of applications like Audacious, Steam, Skype, Transmission, Libreoffice, KDEnlive, Gimp, Virtualbox, Krita, Inkscape, and many more.

Here is an excerpt of some significant version numbers shipped in Netrunner 17.10:

- Linux Kernel 4.10.0-1

- Plasma 5.11.2

- Frameworks 5.35

- Qt 5.9.1

- KDE Applications 17.08

- Firefox 52⁻ESR

- Thunderbird 52.1

Besides the software updates, we added KaoS Isowriter instead of SuseImagewriter and refined the stack overall, including a new default wallpaper.

Netrunner 17.06

It ships with an upgraded stack of KDE Plasma, Frameworks, apps on top of an updated Debian Testing, plus the usual selection of applications like

Audacious, Transmission, Libreoffice, KDEnlive, Steam, Skype, Gimp, Virtualbox, Krita, Inkscape, and many more.

Here is an excerpt of some significant version numbers shipped in Netrunner 17.06:

- Linux Kernel 4.9.0-1

- Plasma 5.10

- Frameworks 5.34

- Qt 5.7.1

- KDE Applications 17.04

- Firefox 52~ESR

- Thunderbird 52.1

Netrunner 17.03

It is known as "Cyclotron" ships with an upgraded KDE software stack plus its usual selection of applications like Libreoffice, KDEnlive, Gimp, Audacious, Steam, etc. Skype, Transmission, Virtualbox, Krita, Inkscape, and many more.

Here are some versions of what is shipped in Netrunner Desktop 17.03:

- Linux Kernel 4.9.0-1

- Plasma 5.9.3

- Frameworks 5.31

- Qt 5.7.1

- KDE Applications 16.12.2

- Firefox 52~ESR

- Thunderbird 45

Netrunner Desktop 17.01

It is known as "Baryon" has jumped from Debian Jessie to the Snapshot "20161211" of Debian Testing, which means the system can be kept on a particular version stack. At the same time, it is also easy to enable the corresponding repositories for continuous updates of Debian Testing.

Netrunner ships with the usual selection of software applications like KDEnlive, Gimp, VLC, LibreOffice, Audacious, Steam, Skype, Transmission, Virtualbox, Krita, Inkscape, and many more.

Here is an overview of what's new in Netrunner Desktop 17.01:

- Debian Testing – Snapshot "20161211"

- Linux Kernel 4.8.0-2

- Plasma 5.8.2

- Frameworks 5.27

- Qt 5.7.1

- KDE Applications 16.08.2

- Firefox 50.0.2

- Thunderbird 45.3

Netrunner Desktop 16.09

It is known as "Avalon" is the full desktop version based on the same stack as Netrunner Core. Both share the same underlying technology, and it features the same KDE Plasma, Frameworks, and KDE Application packages on Debian Stable.

Here is an overview of what's included in Netrunner Desktop 16.09:

- Based on Debian Jessie 8 Stable

- Linux Kernel 4.7

- Plasma 5.7.5

- Frameworks 5.26

- Qt 5.7

- KDE Applications 16.08

- Firefox 49

- Thunderbird 45.3

GARUDA LINUX

Garuda Linux was released on March 26, 2020. Developers around the world develop it. They are founded by Shrinivas Vishnu Kumbhar (India) and SGS (Germany).

It is a Linux-based distribution on the Arch Linux operating system. Garuda Linux is now available in wide range of popular Linux desktop environments, including versions of the KDE Plasma 5 desktop environment. It features a rolling update model using Pacman as its package manager. The term Garuda, originates from Hinduism, which is defined as a divine eagle-like sun bird and the king of birds.

Garuda Linux is a modern Arch-based distribution that focuses on a customized experience. The KDE version offers a beautiful experience while tweaking it with a macOS-like workflow. Of course, if you are an experienced Linux user, you may customize your existing distribution to mimic the same experience. Garuda Linux also provides different variants of its KDE editions, one with preinstalling gaming tools, one for penetration testing, and another as an essential Linux desktop system.

Key Highlights:

- It comes with essential preinstalled GUI tools to make the Arch Linux experience easy.

- Rolling-release distro.

- BTRFS is the default filesystem.

Garuda Linux KDE comes in three variants:

- Dragonized

- Dragonized Gaming

- Dragonized BlackArch

This section is about the KDE Dragonized Edition. It is one of the three highly customized Dragonized variants featuring the Plasma desktop out of four Plasma editions also nine others that feature other desktop environments or window managers.

The KDE Dragonized Edition is modified from the version vanilla by Plasma desktop compared to the slight customizations offered by other distributions. The most of the customizations is the replacement of the typical Plasma shell configuration of a single bottom panel encapsulating a task switcher, system tray, and launcher widget with a configuration uses a top panel rendered by Latte in panel mode that contains the current Plasma default Application Launcher, as well as the Window Buttons, Window Title, Window AppMenu, the Plasma System Tray, and the Event Calendar widgets. Garuda Plasmashell includes a bottom Latte dock. The top panel of Unity in look and behavior, while the overall look of the configuration is very similar to macOS. The configuration of the GUI shell happens to be identical to how we customize Plasma on any distribution.

System requirements:

- Its hardware requirements vary on the Desktop Environment used but are very similar.

Recommended requirements:

- 40 GB storage
- 8 GB RAM

Minimum requirements:

- 30 GB storage
- 4 GB RAM

It also requires a thumbdrive that contains 4GB of space for their standard versions. Its gaming Desktop Environments require a thumbdrive with 8GB storage space available.

Features

Its installation process is done with Calamares, a graphical installer. The rolling release means that the user doesn't need to upgrade/reinstall the whole operating system to keep it up-to-date with the newest release. Pacman handles package management through the command line and front-end UI package manager tools like the preinstalled Pamac. It can configure as either a stable system bleeding edge in line with Arch Linux. Garuda Linux has colorized UI, which comes in various options, with the option to customize the user preferences further.

FEREN OS

Feren OS was created in 2014, its first release in 2015. While the initial release was a complete failure to install, it received a new release in 2016, developed to improve it over time, and addressed the significant issues.

It is a Linux-based operating system mainly based on the Linux Kernel. Its primary goal is to create a unified, user-friendly environment while exposing the underlying advanced technologies. Its mission includes creating an environment where any other application can fit and work with the OS while also working perfectly with the other applications.

Official Editions

Feren OS is a desktop environment that includes Feren's dark theme and Feren's desktop. Feren developers have their own Feren OS Transfer tool, which efficiently transfers data from Windows to Feren OS.

Features:

- Feren OS was on top of Linux Mint. Feren OS takes Ubuntu and makes it user-friendly. It accomplishes this by transforming it into a more ready-to-use desktop than the open source Ubuntu, intended to appeal to a wide range of users.

- It runs on a customized KDE desktop environment that has been fine-tuned for ease of use. KDE is a highly customizable desktop environment that power users often prefer. Feren OS's creator has adopted the adaptable desktop environment to make it more user-friendly for new Linux users.

- There's also Remmina, a remote desktop client, and Krita, a raster graphics editor, in addition to LibreOffice and VLC. The distro includes the Vivaldi web browser and some useful apps such as the Boot-Repair tool and Timeshift, a system restore utility that takes regular incremental snapshots of the file system.

- The distro's pragmatic approach is demonstrated by the inclusion of the proprietary Vivaldi browser. If you don't want to use a closed-source browser, switch to an open source one.

Arch Linux Installation

KDE does not allow login as root directly. If you have installed Arch Linux and you can use it as a root, you should also create a new user and give it sudo privileges for running commands as root. If you have a bare minimum installation of Arch Linux, you probably are logging into a TTY terminal. If you are using another desktop environment, the steps remain the same.

Arch Linux is a Linux distribution created for x86-64 processors. The project attempts to have minimal distribution-specific changes, breakage with updates, be pragmatic over ideological design choices, and focus on customizability rather than user-friendliness.

Pacman

It is a package manager, written primarily for Arch Linux, installing, removing, and updating software packages. Arch Linux uses a rolling model, indicating there are no "major releases" of new versions of the system; a regular system update is all that is required to obtain the latest Arch software; the installation images released every month by the Arch team are simply up-to-date the main system segments.

Arch Linux's supported binary platform is x86_64. The Arch package repositories and User Repository contain 58,000 binary and source packages, which come to Debian's 68,000 packages; however, the two distributions' approaches to packaging differ, making comparisons difficult.

For example, six out of Arch's 58,000 packages include the software AbiWord. Three in the repository replace the canonical Abiword package with an alternative build type or version. In contrast, Debian installs a single version of Abiword across seven packages. The Arch User Repository contains a writer package that installs several document format converters, while Debian provides 20+ converters in its subpackage.

Install KDE on Arch Linux

First, upgrade Arch Linux using the package manager "Pacman" in Arch Linux. Open the terminal application and execute the following command:

```
$ sudo pacman -Syu
```

Now, install the following packages:

- **plasma:** It is a desktop environment for KDE.

- **Sddm:** It is a display manager for KDE plasma.

- **kde-application:** It is for various KDE applications.

- **$ sudo pacman:** S plasma sddm kde-applications.

You will ask to choose the packages, and you can proceed as default values.

Check your current display manager when the installation is finished by executing the following command:

```
$ file ./etc/systemd/system/display-manager.service
```

In this case, the display manager is lightdm. It depends on what you have used while installing Arch Linux.

It would help if you disabled the current display manager, grabbed the name of the display manager from the output, and disabled it by executing the following command:

```
$ sudo systemctl disable lightdm
```

Now enable session manager for kde plasma "sddm" and reboot the system using the command given below.

```
$ sudo systemctl enable sddm
```

and reboot your system,

```
$ reboot
```

The following screen appears. Choose "Plasma and input your password. You will be login to the KDE Plasma Desktop top.

NITRUX

It is a Linux desktop distribution based on Debian. It uses NX Desktop, the Calamares installer, and the NX Firewall on the KDE Plasma 5 desktop environment and KDE Applications.

Nitrux emphasizes the use of AppImages to manage end-user software. Nitrux also does not use the system as its init system; instead, it uses OpenRC.

Nitrux is always up-to-date, using the latest Debian base and to the effort of the KDE Neon developers, who provide the latest stable releases of Plasma. It provides users with the latest MESA drivers from Git and kernels optimized for intensive tasks such as gaming with XanMod and Liquorix.

It is a KDE Plasma + Debian-based Linux distribution that provides features NX Desktop with Plasma desktop with its flavor. It brings the applications based on the Maui desktop. It uses OpenRC as the init system, which is lightweight and brings additional advantages over methods.

Almost after a year, the team informed the release of Nitrux 1.7 with KDE Plasma 5.23 desktop environment, KDE Framework version 5.87, Linux Kernel version 5.14 with other Kernel mods.

Nitrux 1.7 Release

This release presents KDE Plasma Desktop 5.23, KDE Framework version 5.87, KDE Gear 21.08.

The Linux Kernel 5.14 and 5.10 are available to install from the NX repo.

You can install the kernels with Nitrux. It has the latest Liquorix, Xanmod, and Linux Libre kernels and can install separately using the following commands:

```
$ sudo apt install linux-image-xanmod
$ sudo apt install linux-image-libre-lts
```

Application Stack is updated to their respective versions as below,

- LibreOffice 7.2

- Firefox 93.0

- Kdenlive 21.08.2

MX LINUX

It is a midweight Linux operating system based on Debian stable and using core antiX components, with some software created or packaged by the MX community. It was developed between the antiX and former MEPIS communities. The MX "name" came from the M for MEPIS and the X from antiX, acknowledging their roots. The community goal is to produce "a family of operating systems that can combine elegant desktops with high stability and reliable performance." It uses the Xfce desktop environment as its flagship, to which it adds a freestanding KDE Plasma version and, in 2021, a standalone Fluxbox implementation. Other environments can add or are available as "spin-off" ISO images.

History

MX Linux began in December 2013. Developers of antiX joined them, bringing the ISO build system as well as Live-USB/DVD technology. It was initially presented as a version of antiX. It received its DistroWatch page with the release of the first beta (public) of MX-16 on November 2, 2016.

The MX-14 series is based on Debian Stable "Wheezy." It quickly intended to fit onto a CD, limiting the number of applications that could be included and gradual evolution of the MX Tools, a collection of utilities to help users with simple, often complicated, and obscure tasks. MX-15 version moved to the new Debian Stable "Jessie," which means systemd is installed, but the default init is sysvinit. The size limitation lifted, enabling the developers to present a complete product.

The MX-14 version is based on Debian Stable "Jessie," but with many applications backported and added from other sources. There are further refinements to MX Tools, the import of advanced antiX developments, expanded support, and a completely new icon/theme/wallpaper collection. MX-16.1 version collected all bug fixes and improvements since the MX-16 version, added a new theme, upgraded and streamlined MX Tools, revised documentation, and added new translations. MX-17 version changed its base to Debian 9 and brought upgraded artwork, new MX Tools, improved Live operation via antiX, and other changes. MX-18 continued the development of MX Tools, enabled whole disk encryption, introduced a new kernel, and added grub themes, splash functionality using MX Boot options artwork, and improved localization. MX-19 version upgraded its base to Debian 10, and it is default desktop to Xfce 4.14. It is characterized by new tools, artwork, documentation, localization, and technical features. Version MX-21 was released on October 21, 2021. It is based on Debian 11 and is available as Xfce, KDE, or Fluxbox versions.

KDE Plasma is a unique and powerful desktop environment available for MX Linux users. When compared to other desktops available for MX Linux, it can be argued that KDE requires more compute resources to run a good deal of user knowledge and experience to customize.

Here we show you how to install and use KDE Desktop Environment on MX Linux 21/19.x. We will use the MX Package Installer method or choose direct apt installation via task-KDE-desktop. Follow these steps in the next section to install KDE Desktop Environment on MX Linux 21/19.

Desktop Environments

Besides the fast and medium resource default XFCE desktop environment, MX Linux has two other desktop editions:

A free-standing "Fluxbox" version with shallow resource usage was released on October 21, 2021.

A "KDE" was released on August 16, 2020, Advanced Hardware Support enabled (64-bit only) version of MX featuring the KDE/Plasma Desktop and currently features a long-term supported Linux 5.10.x AHS kernel.

In addition, an "XFCE" Advanced Hardware Support was released with newer graphics drivers, 5.10 kernel, and firmware for very recent hardware.

Minimum System Requirements:

- 8.5 GB hard disk for installation.

- Need 1 GB RAM for i386 & AMD64 architectures.

- Support bootable CD-DVD drive or a USB stick.

- A modern i686 Intel or AMD processor.

Recommended:

- Need 20 GB of hard disk space, SSD for faster performance.

- 2 GB of RAM and modern i686 Intel or AMD processor. Multi-core for good performance.

- Support 3D-capable video card for 3D desktop with SoundBlaster, AC97, or HDA-compatible sound card.

- For use as a LiveUSB, 8 GB free if using persistence.

Update System

You should update all the preinstalled packages on the system to the latest releases to avoid issues.

```
$ sudo apt update && sudo apt upgrade -y
```

Also, check and apply any minor distribution system updates available.

```
$ sudo apt dist-upgrade -y
```

Consider a system reboot once the upgrades are done.

```
$ sudo reboot
```

Install KDE Desktop Environment on MX Linux version 21/19:

- The quickest installation method for KDE Desktop Environment on MX Linux 21/19 is the Package Manager path. Start Package Manager application on your Desktop.

- Search using keywords "KDE."

- Choose "KDE" environment and any other package you like.

- Use "Install" to begin the download and installation process now, accept the installation of extra packages by choosing "OK."

- When you want to continue, answer yes with the y key and choose the default display manager.

- KDE and its packages will be installed on the MX Linux system.

- Reboot your machine.

- Choose the KDE Desktop Environment at the login screen.

- You can confirm that MX Linux is booted to the KDE Desktop Environment on the system.

Features

MX Linux has essential tools like a graphic installer handling UEFI computers. It is a GUI-based method to change a Linux kernel and other core programs.

It includes MX Tools, a suite of user-oriented utilities, many of which were developed specifically for MX. Some forked from existing antiX applications or existing antiX applications; a couple was imported with permission from outside sources.

A popular one is MX-snapshot, a GUI tool to remaster a live session or installation into a single. ISO file. The "cloned" image is bootable from a disk or USB flash drive, maintaining settings, allowing an installation to be completely backed up, and distributed with the minimal administrative effort since an advanced method of copying the file system uses bind-mounts performing the "heavy lifting."

ROSA LINUX

It is a Linux operating system distribution developed by the Russian company "LLC NTC IT ROSA." It is available in three different editions: ROSA Desktop Fresh, ROSA Enterprise Desktop, and ROSA Enterprise

Linux Server. Its desktop editions come bundled with closed-source software such as multimedia codecs, Adobe Flash Player, and Steam. ROSA Desktop Fresh version R11.1. The latest desktop release on April 23, 2020, is available with four different desktop environments: KDE Plasma 4 KDE Plasma 5 Xfce LXQt. It also contains open source software developed in-house by ROSA. It has been certified by the Ministry of Defense of Russia. ROSA originated as a fork of now-defunct French distribution Mandriva Linux and has been developed independently. It was founded in early 2010. Its first version of its operating system in December 2010 and initially targeted enterprise users only, but in late 2012, ROSA started its end-user-oriented distribution, Desktop Fresh. Mandriva 2011 was also based on ROSA. Also, Magos Linux is based on ROSA. Although its prominent popularity is in the Russian language market, ROSA Desktop also received favorable reviews from several non-Russian online publications. German technology website Golem.de praised ROSA for its stability and hardware support, while LinuxInsider.com called ROSA "a real Powerhouse."

It is a Russian Linux distribution featuring a customized KDE desktop and the working environment. This product comes with commercial support.

Rosa Version Release

ROSA R6 "Desktop Fresh LXQt"

The release of ROSA R6 "Desktop Fresh LXQt" edition is a lightweight edition with features of the LXQt desktop for the first time using the LXQt desktop environment. Up to Desktop Fresh R5, we released light editions based on LXDE. Hence, LXDE is based on GTK+ 2 library stack, which has not gotten significant updates since 2011. All new features are implemented in the GTK+ 3 series. A group of volunteers still develops the old GTK+ 2-based LXDE, but their progress is not as significant. In particular, there's no significant difference in LXDE components between LXDE editions of ROSA Desktop Fresh R4 and Fresh R5. Still, our distribution has given a "Fresh" word name, so we decided to provide a new desktop environment an opportunity. And after several months of experiments, integration work, and bug fixes, we are ready to present a new edition of ROSA Desktop Fresh, which is based on "LXQt." Continue to the release notes for further information.

ROSA R6 "Desktop Fresh LXQt"

The release of ROSA R6 "Desktop Fresh LXQt" edition is a lightweight edition with features of the LXQt desktop for the first time using the LXQt desktop environment. Up to Desktop Fresh R5, we released light editions based on LXDE. Hence, LXDE is based on GTK+ 2 library stack, which has not gotten significant updates since 2011. All new features are implemented in the GTK+ 3 series. A group of volunteers still develops the old GTK+ 2-based LXDE, but their progress is not as significant. In particular, there's no significant difference in LXDE components between LXDE editions of ROSA Desktop Fresh R4 and Fresh R5. Still, our distribution has given a "Fresh" word name, so we decided to provide a new desktop environment an opportunity. And after several months of experiments, integration work, and bug fixes, we are ready to present a new edition of ROSA Desktop Fresh, which is based on "LXQt."

ROSA R7 "Desktop Fresh GNOME"

The release of this edition is a desktop Linux distribution featuring a customized GNOME 3.16 desktop: "The ROSA company presents ROSA Desktop Fresh GNOME R7." It is a distribution from the ROSA Desktop Fresh family with the GNOME version 3 desktop environment. The distribution presents an extensive collection of games, emulators, and the Steam platform package, with standard suites of audio and video, including the newest version of Skype communications software. Other modern video formats are also supported. Also, it includes the fresh LibreOffice version using new gray icons, which contains GNOME 3.16 with a new user-friendly interface and a system tray. We have replaced the old Elementary theme with a new Korora theme for GNOME Shell and EvoPop for GTK+.

ROSA R8

It has been released unlike the previous versions of ROSA, and this is provided in separate variants featuring the GNOME 3.16, KDE version 4.14, KDE Plasma 5.7, and MATE 1.12 desktop environments.

ROSA Desktop Fresh R8 is a distribution in a constantly changing Linux world. Based on the ROSA 2014.1 platform, the last release is a stable release with two years of extended support.

ROSA Desktop Fresh R8 has features four desktop environments:

- **KDE 4:** Regular version, recommended for home users.

- **GNOME 3:** Simple and easy to use.

- **Plasma 5:** New version of KDE.

It's recommended only for Linux enthusiasts because it's not as stable as KDE 4; MATE is fast and lightweight for older hardware.

ROSA R8.1 This version is a bug-fix update for the KDE edition only, while the remaining flavors such as GNOME, MATE, and Plasma stay at version R8 by launching updated ROSA Fresh R8.1. ROSA Fresh R8.1 release is made for users who need a stable LTS platform on modern hardware. It contains all patches and software updates for Intel Skylake chipset and similar modern chipsets, and kernel 4.9.x is available right out of the box. ROSA Fresh R8.1 includes many bug fixes, primarily for fixing network issues and some installation problems. The essential features and bug fixes are several fixes for installation and booting problems in live mode on some Linux kernel 4.9.x LTS; Mesa 13.0.2 with OpenGL 4.5 to run modern games with free drivers.

Distribution Release: ROSA R9
The ROSA R9 version comes in two desktop variants: KDE 4 or Plasma desktop 5.9. It is the first release based on the new package platform 2016.1. It targeted mainly at Linux advocates eager to try new software. According to the updated policy, the R9 version of the ROSA distribution will have four years of technical support. The technological changes compared to ROSA R8 are most of the system libraries, compilers, and system/user software were updated to their new versions (glibc, boost, GCC, Clang); new additions to the repositories were made, e.g., LDC (the D language compiler), Meson (a powerful open source build system); added a glibc patch, drastically boosting the load speed of the dynamic shared objects (DSO).

Distribution Release: ROSA R9 "LXQt"
ROSA R9 "LXQt" edition is a desktop-focused Linux distribution with the lightweight LXQt 0.11 desktop. LXQt is the lightest and ascetic ROSA R9 edition especially designed for machines that are not rich in features such as netbooks and for users who like an immediate reaction to any action. It will be good even if you have 512 MB of RAM. It specifics of LXQt in ROSA R9: all LXQt components are based on the freshest 0.11 branch with ROSA theme, without compositing the desktop effects. We can use NewMoon (PaleMoon) web browser compatible with Firefox ESR, which is used as a basis. It consumes fewer resources; default installation includes some additional components for Internet users such as Pidgin, qBitTorrent, Trojitá; the nomacs image viewer is installed by default. It provides basic image manipulation facilities; Rosa Media Player and Audacious are included.

Distribution Release: ROSA R11

ROSA R11 is a new stable version from the project that develops a set of desktop-oriented distributions. The latest release is available in four variants featuring such as

- KDE 4

- KDE Plasma

- LXDE

- Xfce desktops

Some of the improvements include like updated such as,

- Linux kernel 4.15.

- Updated desktops, i.e., KDE Plasma 5.14.4.1, LXQt 0.14.0 and Xfce 4.13.2.

- Support for installing the system on M.2.

- Support NVME SSD storage devices and added file system support for FfFS flash drives to its installer.

- It has improved graphic subsystem when ROSA is used as a guest system in virtual machines based on KVM and Hyper-V.

- It has added firmware to installation images to support Epson scanners; the system nowadays creates a universal initrd instead of a hardware-specific one by default.

- The new btrfs-progs 4.19.1 now includes support for the zstd compression algorithm.

ALT KWORKSTATION

It is a solution for organizing end-user workplaces and is suitable for use in the office and at home. The distribution can use in the Active Directory infrastructure and a heterogeneous ALT Server network. The system can use to solve a wide range of tasks such as in a browser, with email, for instant messaging, creation and editing of texts, spread sheets, presentations, work with video and sound files, complex graphics, and animations. It is an operating system with a Plasma desktop and application suite designed for both office and home workplace. Persons can freely use the downloaded version with legal entities for testing, but production use requires acquiring licenses or signing a license agreement in written form.

The free software in these images can be acquired as src: rpm packages and git repos.

openSUSE

It comes in following two versions:

- Leap is stable with regular releases with LTS versions of Linux, Qt, and Plasma.

- Tumbleweed is a rolling distribution with the latest versions of all packages.

openSUSE Is a KDE Patron

KDE is a technology that creates free, open source software for desktop and portable computing. Plasma, which KDE also makes, is one of the graphical desktop environments of openSUSE. The latest version of Plasma 5 is a fresh, elegant, and powerful desktop for beginners and advanced users. Its software is not limited to a desktop environment. The software made by the community includes:

- Plasma for the graphical desktop;

- A collection of various applications such as communication, work, education, entertainment, including famous programs like Kate text editor;

- Additional high-quality applications, such as digiKam and Krita;

- KDE Frameworks, a series of modules to quickly build new applications upon.

What thing makes KDE unique on openSUSE:

- It has a professional team that spends time fixing bugs so that you can work on KDE.

- It has an active, experienced community team who bring multiple points of view and different interests to the project so that KDE software on openSUSE meets users' needs.

- It stimulates the openSUSE to develop, evolve, and progress.

Obtain KDE Software on openSUSE Using a Burned CD/DVD

KDE is preselected on installations from the CD/DVD, so click through the building. If you prefer to download, burn the Live KDE image to a CD or a USB stick. All the same, software is available online through YaST Software Management.

The KDE Platform has a wide range of applications, some of which have constantly been modified since the beginning of the KDE in 1996. Its applications are easy to learn due to the look and design across applications. These applications are fast and reliable by high integration and sharing of components with another workspace. These are the default tools recommended by openSUSE for daily tasks such as,

It offers you the familiarity of the popular browser Firefox and improvements like the KDE file dialog for saving, uploading content, matching theming, and functional bookmarks.

Its attention makes LibreOffice that widely used office suite, fit right in with your desktop.

- Dolphin File Manager gives fast and powerful file management features, whether it's your hard disk, a memory stick, or a remote computer.

- Okular's broad file format support ensures that you can read whatever is on your computer if you want any other PDF reader because of its lightning startup time and support for advanced PDF forms and highlighting features.

- DigiKam is the powerful photo manager on Linux. It makes it easy to share shots on photography and social networking sites like Facebook, Flickr, PicasaWeb, and SmugMug. Prolific snappers application can keep track of thousands of shots and various ways to search for images and appreciate its high performance when viewing thumbnails or editing images. Also, high-end photographers recognize its strong support for many RAW formats and high-bit depth editing.

Linux is the free operating system, and there are naturally many alternatives available to suit your taste, both from the KDE Software Collection (such as Konqueror, KOffice) and other providers. You can use KDE applications under different desktop environments with no loss of functionality.

CHAPTER SUMMARY

So these were some of the top KDE-based Linux distros. As you can see, there is a whole variety of distros specializing in different areas, so you can pick any that resonates with your needs and requirements. For example, go with Fedora or Arch if you are looking for KDE with access to all the features as soon as they are released. It provides a heavily customized KDE desktop but is filled with valuable features and welcomes new users.

Appraisal

Ubuntu and other Linux distro systems took the open source and the IT world by storm in the early years. The miniature operating system has grown into a fully-featured desktop and server offering that has won users' hearts everywhere. Besides the solid technical platform and impressive dedication to quality, KDE distros also enjoy success because of their vast community of enthusiastic users who help support, document, and test every point of the Ubuntu landscape.

In your hands, you have an official, qualified guide to this unique operating system. Each of us working on this book has shown a high level of technical competence and a willingness to share this knowledge. We have gathered together to create a book that offers a solid understanding of the essential points of Ubuntu as well as various other distros such as Fedora, openSUSE, Manjaro.

KDE is the distro that has become the most popular, and arguably, one of the best-loved Linux distributions. K desktop environment is a desktop working platform designed by KDE with a graphical user interface (GUI) released in an open source package. When KDE was first released, it acquired the name Kool desktop environment, abbreviated as K desktop environment. In this book, we are working with KDE Neon, a software repository that uses Ubuntu LTS as a core.

Most KDE software is written in C++ using the Qt toolkit. The prior experience with these programming languages is helpful, but you don't need to be a C++ programmer to get started!

KDE is the most popular desktop environment out there. Many popular Linux distros use KDE as their default desktop environment, and it has some popular forks, such as openSUSE. You may also refer to it as the "Plasma" desktop. Even though it's not always a primary choice, it is highly customizable and highly lightweight.

DOI: 10.1201/9781003309406-6

KDE was created to be easy to use and customizable. Its user interface aims to provide a unique experience. Unfortunately, another desktop environment, GNOME, is not a lightweight desktop environment. So, it's not good to choose to go with if you want to install a Linux distribution on older computers or systems with less than 4 Gigs of RAM.

It's good to try KDE Plasma rather than GNOME because KDE is lighter and faster than GNOME, and it's more customizable. GNOME is for OS X converts who are not used to anything customizable, but KDE is a delight for everyone else.

Your system requires 64-bit PC (Intel or AMD) 2GB memory to install KDE Neon. 10GB disk space.

But it is good to see that KDE is focusing on the performance side of things with their latest KDE Plasma 5 release. So, if you want to use a good user experience that looks different from a basic layout, KDE should be the perfect pick. KDE's major distros are Kubuntu, Fedora KDE, openSUSE, though its other distros also have good features.

This book can vary in coverage over various topics. It is intentional. Any other book does not cover some topics, and they deserve deep coverage here. There are some topics that power users master. Other topics are things the power users should know about. They can understand some history, some other options, or have what they need to listen to further discussions with different technical views without being completely confused.

This book is planned for intermediate and advanced users or those who want to become middle and advanced users. Our goal is to give you the right direction to help you enter the higher stages by telling you to use as many tools and ideas as possible. We give you some thoughts and methods to consider so you can seek out more. Although the contents are for intermediate to advanced users, new users who pay attention will benefit from each chapter where all chapters are related. The central pointer is that more detailed or related information is provided at the end of each chapter.

This book helps you to learn these skills and tells you how to learn more about your system, Linux, with the software included Ubuntu distros with the desktop environment. Most importantly, it enables you to overcome your fear of the system by telling you more about it and how it works. You can also install the other Linux distros like Fedora, openSUSE, Manjora, etc.

This book is not a pure reference book and it also properly guides you with step-by-step procedures for performing tasks. The book is organized by topics and includes many useful commands.

Chapter 1 contains the basic understanding of the system's installation and how it is different from other Linux distro systems and some specific terms like GUI, CLI, and TUI. It describes the vast resources available to support this book. You will get a brief summary of KDE's history, features, and some pros and cons as well.

Chapter 2 contains a quick review of the KDE installation, describes valuable commands such as apt-get snapd and gives you brief knowledge of the user interface of the KDE system.

Chapter 3 provides a quick review of the installation of KDE-based applications like KDailog, Elisa, KOrganizer, Konqueror, K3b, Kcolorchooser, Krita, Kwalletmanager, Kate, and also describes their features and various components relating to the user interface.

Chapter 4 provides a quick review of QT programming, its history, Software Architecture, various binding languages of Qt programming, and the basics of developing apps for KDE and Kirigami components.

Chapter 5 provides you with knowledge of the other KDE-based Linux distros like Kubuntu, Manjaro KDE, Fedora KDE Plasma Desktop Edition, Netrunner, Garuda Linux, Feren OS, Arch Linux Installation, Nitrux, MX Linux, ROSA Linux, ALT KWorkstation, openSUSE, etc.

This book will be most helpful to you if you are working on a KDE distro with KDE Plasma as its default desktop environment or another operating system.

Bibliography

About Qt – Qt Wiki. (n.d.). About Qt – Qt Wiki; wiki.qt.io. Retrieved July 11, 2022, from https://wiki.qt.io/About_Qt

APT (software) – Wikipedia. (1998, March 31). APT (Software) – Wikipedia; en.wikipedia.org. https://en.wikipedia.org/wiki/APT_(software)#:~:text=Advanced%20package%20tool%2C%20or%20APT%2C%20is%20a%20free-software,software%20on%20Debian%2C%20and%20Debian%20-based%20Linux%20distributions

DebugPoint.com. (n.d.). DebugPoint.Com; www.debugpoint.com. Retrieved July 11, 2022, from https://www.debugpoint.com/

Embedded Software Development Tools | Cross Platform IDE | Qt Creator. (n.d.). Embedded Software Development Tools | Cross Platform IDE | Qt Creator; www.qt.io. Retrieved July 11, 2022, from https://www.qt.io/product/development-tools

Herrera, U. (2022, July 1). *Nitrux — #YourNextOS — Boldly Different.* Nitrux — #YourNextOS; nxos.org. https://nxos.org/

https://distrowatch.com/

Installing KDE Neon – KDE UserBase Wiki. (n.d.). Installing KDE Neon – KDE UserBase Wiki; userbase.kde.org. Retrieved July 11, 2022, from https://userbase.kde.org/Installing_KDE_neon

K Desktop Environment 1 – Wikipedia. (1998, July 12). K Desktop Environment 1 – Wikipedia; en.wikipedia.org. https://en.wikipedia.org/wiki/K_Desktop_Environment_1

K Desktop Environment 2 – Wikipedia. (2000, October 23). K Desktop Environment 2 – Wikipedia; en.wikipedia.org. https://en.wikipedia.org/wiki/K_Desktop_Environment_2

K Desktop Environment 3 – Wikipedia. (2002, April 3). K Desktop Environment 3 – Wikipedia; en.wikipedia.org. https://en.wikipedia.org/wiki/K_Desktop_Environment_3

K Desktop Environment 4 – Wikipedia. (2002, April 3). K Desktop Environment 3 – Wikipedia; en.wikipedia.org. https://en.wikipedia.org/wiki/K_Desktop_Environment_4

KDE – Wikipedia. (1996, October 14). KDE – Wikipedia; en.wikipedia.org. https://en.wikipedia.org/wiki/KDE#:~:text=KDE%20is%20an%20international%20free%20software%20community%20that,collaborative%20work%20on%20this%20kind%20of%20software.%20

KDE – Wikipedia. (1996, October 14). KDE – Wikipedia; en.wikipedia.org. https://en.wikipedia.org/wiki/KDE

KDE Neon – Wikipedia. (2016, June 8). KDE Neon – Wikipedia; en.wikipedia.org. https://en.wikipedia.org/wiki/KDE_neon

KDE Plasma | Linux Wiki | Fandom. (n.d.). Linux Wiki; linux.fandom.com. Retrieved July 11, 2022, from https://linux.fandom.com/wiki/KDE_Plasma#:~:text=K%20Desktop%20Environment%20%28KDE%29%20was%20founded%20in%201996,of%20the%20applications%20looked%2C%20felt%2C%20or%20worked%20alike

KDE Plasma 5 – Wikipedia. (2014, July 15). KDE Plasma 5 – Wikipedia; en.wikipedia.org. https://en.wikipedia.org/wiki/KDE_Plasma_5

Kubuntu – Wikipedia. (2005, April 8). Kubuntu – Wikipedia; en.wikipedia.org. https://en.wikipedia.org/wiki/Kubuntu#:~:text=Kubuntu%20%28%2F%20k%CA%8A%CB%88b%CA%8Antu%CB%90%20%2F%20kuu-BUUN-too%29%20is%20an%20official,Ubuntu%20project%2C%20Kubuntu%20uses%20the%20same%20underlying%20systems

Microsoft Visual Studio – Wikipedia. (2022, February 15). Microsoft Visual Studio – Wikipedia; en.wikipedia.org. https://en.wikipedia.org/wiki/Microsoft_Visual_Studio

Package ISO Release – Nitrux – OSDN. (2022, July 1). Package ISO Release – Nitrux – OSDN; osdn.net. https://osdn.net/projects/nitrux/releases/p18379#:~:text=Nitrux%20is%20a%20Linux%20desktop%

20distribution%20directly%20based,the%20use%20of%20 AppImages%20to%20manage%20end-user%20software

Plasma – KDE.org. (n.d.). Plasma – KDE.Org; www.kde.com. Retrieved July 11, 2022, from http://www.kde.com/plasma-desktop

Qbs. (n.d.). Qbs; qbs.io. Retrieved July 11, 2022, from https://qbs.io/ docs/overview/#:~:text=Qbs%20is%20an%20all-in-one%20tool%20 that%20generates%20a,and%20multi-core%20systems%20to%20 achieve%20maximum%20build%20parallelization

QLabel – Qt for Python. (n.d.). QLabel — Qt for Python; doc.qt.io. Retrieved July 11, 2022, from https://doc.qt.io/qtforpython-5/ PySide2/QtWidgets/QLabel.html

Qt (software) – Wikipedia. (1995, May 20). Qt (Software) – Wikipedia; en.wikipedia.org. https://en.wikipedia.org/wiki/Qt_(software)#:~:text= Qt%20%28pronounced%20%22cute%22%29%20is%20a%20cross-platform%20software%20for,a%20native%20application%20 with%20native%20capabilities%20and%20speed

Qt Documentation | Home. (n.d.). Qt Documentation | Home; doc.qt.io. Retrieved July 11, 2022, from https://doc.qt.io/

Qt Quick – Qt Wiki. (n.d.). Qt Quick – Qt Wiki; wiki.qt.io. Retrieved July 11, 2022, from https://wiki.qt.io/Qt_Quick

ROSA Linux: App Reviews, Features, Pricing & Download | AlternativeTo

Soft32. (2007, January 5). *Download GNU Make 3.81.* Download GNU Make 3.81; gnu-make.soft32.com. https://gnu-make.soft32.com/

team, K. N. (n.d.). *KDE neon.* KDE Neon; neon.kde.org. Retrieved July 11, 2022, from https://neon.kde.org/download

Xcode – Wikipedia. (2003, October 23). Xcode – Wikipedia; en.wikipedia. org. https://en.wikipedia.org/wiki/Xcode#:~:text=Xcode%20is%20 Apple%27s%20integrated%20development%20environment%20 %28IDE%29%20for,free%20of%20charge%20for%20macOS%20 Monterey%20users.%20

Index

Printed in the United States
by Baker & Taylor Publisher Services